Believe First Achieve Next

OrangeBooks Publication

1st Floor, Rajhans Arcade, Mall Road, Kohka, Bhilai, Chhattisgarh 490020
Website: **www.orangebooks.in**

First Edition, 2026

ISBN: 978-93-7426-973-2

Price: Rs. 359.00

Printed in India

BELIEVE FIRST
Achieve Next

Confidence is the Key

The Ultimate Success Guide for LIC Agents

Sathya Prakash Urs S N

M.Sc., MBA (Ph.D.)

Motivational Speaker | Trainer | Mentor

OrangeBooks Publication

www.orangebooks.in

Dedication

This book is respectfully dedicated to all LIC Agents who work tirelessly to protect families and secure their future.

Your profession is not merely selling policies — it is giving financial life support to families during their most difficult times. Because of your efforts, many children continue their education, many parents live with dignity, and many homes remain stable even in the absence of the earning member.

I gratefully dedicate this book to my teachers and trainers who guided me with knowledge, discipline, and the right values. Their teachings shaped my thinking, built my confidence, and inspired me to share what I have learned with others. Whatever I am today is a reflection of their guidance.

I lovingly dedicate this work to my beloved parents, whose blessings, sacrifices, and moral values became the foundation of my life. Their encouragement has always been my greatest strength and motivation.

Finally, I dedicate this book to my family members who stood beside me with patience, support, and understanding throughout this journey. Their faith and encouragement made this effort possible.

May this book motivate every LIC agent to work with honesty, confidence, and a service mindset — and may every family live with financial security and peace of mind.

Sathya Prakash Urs S N M.Sc., MBA (Ph.D.)

LIC Chief Organiser

Motivational Speaker | Trainer | Mentor

Preface

India is a country of dreams. Every father dreams about his children's education. Every mother dreams about a safe family. Every employee dreams about a peaceful retirement. Yet, one unexpected event can destroy years of hard work and planning.

In such situations, a Life Insurance Agent is not merely a salesperson. He is a protector of families, a planner of futures, and a silent guardian of financial security. A doctor saves a patient's life, but a life insurance agent saves the family's life even after the earning member is no more.

Unfortunately, many LIC agents enter this profession without proper guidance, confidence, and communication skills. They struggle not because LIC products are weak, but because they are not trained in understanding people, building trust, and creating financial awareness. Insurance is not a product-selling business; it is a relationship-building service.

This book is written with a simple purpose — to transform an LIC agent into a respected financial advisor. Inside these pages, you will not only learn how to approach a customer but also how to understand human psychology, how to create need, how to explain security, and how to confidently close a policy with honesty and dignity.

Success in LIC does not depend on luck, contacts, or market conditions. It depends on daily activity, positive mindset, discipline, and service attitude. When an agent starts thinking "I am helping families" instead of "I am selling policies," everything changes. Customers start trusting. Conversations become easier. Performance improves naturally.

Remember, people do not buy insurance because they love paying premiums. They buy insurance because they love their family.

If this book helps even one agent stand confidently in front of a client, explain the value of protection, and secure one family's future, its purpose is fulfilled.

Let us work together to create a society where no family suffers financially due to the absence of proper planning.

Believe First — Achieve Next

Sathya Prakash Urs S N M.Sc., MBA (Ph.D.)

LIC Chief Organiser

Motivational Speaker | Trainer | Mentor

Acknowledgement

I express my sincere gratitude to the Life Insurance Corporation of India for creating a noble platform where ordinary individuals can become financial protectors of society. The values of trust, service, and long-term commitment taught by LIC have inspired me to write this book.

I am deeply thankful to all senior development officers, mentors, and successful agents whose real-life experiences helped me understand the practical challenges faced in the field. Their dedication to guiding customers and supporting families has been a great learning source.

My heartfelt thanks to every customer who trusted an LIC agent and believed in financial protection. Each conversation, each policy, and each family story has contributed to the knowledge shared in this book.

I would especially like to thank my parents for their blessings and my family members for their encouragement and patience throughout this journey. Their faith in me made this work possible.

Finally, I thank every reader and LIC agent who picks up this book with a desire to learn and improve. If these pages help you build confidence, serve families better, and achieve success with honesty, my effort will be truly rewarded.

Sathya Prakash Urs S N M.Sc., MBA (Ph.D.)

LIC Chief Organizer

Motivational Speaker | Trainer | Mentor

About The Author

Sathya Prakash Urs S N (M.Sc., MBA (PhD)) is an Assistant Professor, LIC Chief Organiser, Motivational Speaker, Trainer, and Mentor dedicated to developing confidence and professional skills among life insurance agents and young professionals.

With a strong academic background and practical field experience, he has guided many LIC agents on communication, customer psychology, and relationship-based selling. His training focuses on transforming agents from policy sellers into trusted financial advisors by emphasising ethics, discipline, and a service mindset.

He believes that the life insurance profession is not merely a business but a social responsibility that protects families from financial hardship. Through seminars, workshops, and personal mentoring, he has inspired agents to work with confidence and integrity.

His mission is to create financially aware communities where every family understands the importance of protection planning and long-term security.

This book, *Believe First — Achieve Next*, is written to provide practical guidance, motivation, and step-by-step methods for LIC agents to improve performance and build a respected career.

"When agents grow in knowledge and confidence, families grow in security."

Contents

CHAPTER 01

THE NOBLE PROFESSION OF LIFE INSURANCE

Every profession earns income, but only a few professions earn blessings. The life insurance profession is one among them.

A teacher gives knowledge.

A doctor saves a patient.

A farmer feeds the nation.

And a life insurance agent protects a family's future.

Most people misunderstand the role of a Life Insurance agent. They think an agent is a person who comes to sell a policy and collect premiums. But the truth is very different. A life insurance agent is a financial protector who stands silently behind a family and supports them during the most painful and unexpected moments of life.

Imagine a situation where a family suddenly loses its earning member. Income stops immediately, but expenses do not stop. Children's education continues, house rent or loan continues, food expenses continue, and medical needs continue. At that time, relatives may offer emotional support to the family, but only proper financial planning can support them in practical terms. That support comes from life insurance.

The cheque that reaches a family after a claim is not just money. It is the school fees for a child. It is the monthly groceries for a mother. It is a dignity for aged parents. It is hope during helplessness. The person who made that possible is the life insurance agent.

Unfortunately, many agents themselves underestimate their profession. When an agent feels he is "just selling a policy," his confidence decreases. When he realises he is "protecting a family," his confidence automatically increases. Confidence does not come from product knowledge alone; it comes from purpose.

Insurance is not purchased because people like to pay premiums. People purchase insurance because they love their family and do not want them to suffer in their absence. Therefore, a Life Insurance agent should never hesitate while approaching a customer. He is not asking for a favour; he is offering security.

Rejection is a common part of this profession. A customer may postpone, avoid, or say no. But a "no" does not mean the customer hates you. It only means the customer has not yet understood the importance of protection. The duty of an agent is not to force a policy but to create awareness.

When awareness increases, acceptance naturally follows.

A successful Life Insurance agent works with three principles — honesty, patience, and service. Honesty builds trust. Patience builds relationships. Service builds long-term business. Policies may lapse, but relationships never lapse. When a customer trusts an agent, he not only buys a policy but also refers relatives and friends.

This profession rewards consistency more than talent. An ordinary person with daily effort can become a top performer, while a talented person without discipline may fail. The secret of success is simple: meet people, understand their needs, and guide them sincerely.

Never feel ashamed to say you are a Life Insurance agent. Say it with pride. You are not disturbing people; you are protecting their future.

Always remember:

You are not selling a document.

You are delivering peace of mind.

When you start working with this belief, your fear reduces, your confidence improves, and your performance increases automatically. The moment you change your thinking, the profession changes for you.

The day you understand the value of your role, customers will also understand it.

This is not just a career.

This is a responsibility to society.

And every time you complete a policy, you are not closing a sale — you are opening security for a family.

CHAPTER 02

FROM POLICY SELLER TO FAMILY PROTECTOR

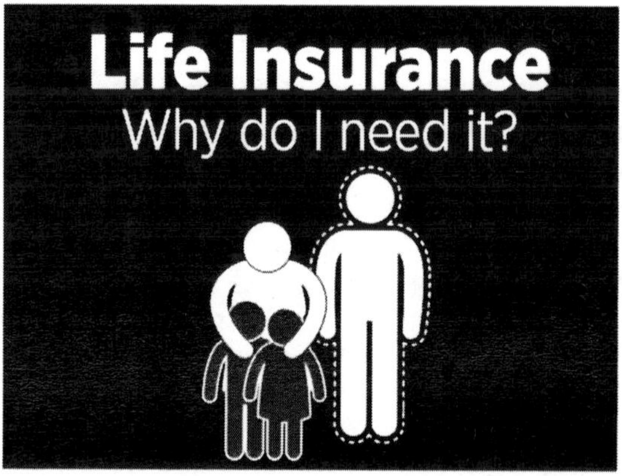

One of the biggest reasons many Life Insurance agents struggle in the beginning is the wrong self-image. They believe, "I am going to sell a policy." The moment an agent thinks like a salesperson, fear automatically starts—fear of rejection, hesitation to approach people, and tension while speaking to customers.

But a simple change in thinking can completely transform an agent's career.

You are not a policy seller.

You are a family protector.

A policy seller talks about the premium.

A family protector talks about responsibility.

A policy seller explains plan features.

A family protector explains family security.

Customers can easily avoid a salesperson, but they always listen to a genuine advisor.

When an agent visits a client only to complete a target, the customer feels pressure. However, when the agent visits to discuss the future of the family, the customer feels concern and care. People may doubt your product, but they will not doubt your intention if they feel you genuinely care for them.

Insurance is not a product-first conversation. It is a person-first conversation.

Instead of starting with plans, start with life. Ask about the family, children, parents, work, responsibilities, and future goals. Slowly, the customer will open up. Once the customer begins to speak about his family, he becomes emotionally involved. At that point, he is not talking to an agent — he is talking to a well-wisher.

Every earning member has four major responsibilities:

- Children's education
- Family monthly expenses
- Loan or liabilities
- Retirement security

If these four areas are not protected, the family becomes financially vulnerable. The role of a Life Insurance agent is to help the customer see this reality clearly.

Never begin your discussion with a policy chart. Begin with a simple question:

"If your income stops tomorrow, how long can your family manage comfortably?"

This one question makes the customer think seriously. When thinking begins, need begins. When need begins, acceptance begins.

Remember, customers rarely buy insurance because of calculations. They buy because of realisation.

Many agents talk too much about returns, bonuses, and maturity. While these are important, they are secondary. The primary purpose of life insurance is protection. Investment is a benefit, but protection is the foundation.

An agent should act like a doctor. A doctor does not administer medicine before a diagnosis. Similarly, an agent should not suggest a plan before a clear understanding the family's situation. First, understand income, expenses, dependents, and future goals. Then recommend a suitable solution.

Another common mistake is fear of rejection. Rejection is not failure. Rejection is part of awareness building. Many customers who initially say "not now" later become your best clients if you maintain the relationship and follow up politely.

Service mindset is the real secret of long-term success. After issuing a policy, continue contact with the customer — birthday wishes, policy reminders, and periodic reviews. When the customer feels you are available even after receiving commission, trust becomes permanent.

When trust becomes permanent, business becomes automatic.

A successful Life Insurance agent does not chase customers. Customers start calling the agent.

This transformation happens when you stop thinking about selling and start thinking about serving.

Always keep this belief in your mind:

You are not requesting a customer to help you earn commission.

You are helping a customer protect his family.

The day you start working with this belief, your confidence in conversation will improve. Your body language will become natural. Your words will become convincing. And most importantly, your profession will give you satisfaction along with income.

A policy seller looks for a signature.

A family protector looks for a secure future.

Decide today which one you want to become.

CHAPTER 03

UNDERSTANDING THE REAL ROLE OF A LIFE INSURANCE AGENT

Many Life Insurance agents believe their job is to explain a plan and collect a premium. Because of this misunderstanding, they speak continuously about tables, terms, bonuses, and maturity values. Unfortunately, customers often lose interest within a few minutes.

The real role of a Life Insurance agent is not to explain policies.

The real role of a Life Insurance agent is to guide financial decisions.

A customer does not need a walking brochure. A customer needs a trusted advisor.

When a person invites you for a meeting, he is not inviting you to read the plan details. He is inviting you to help him make a safe decision for his family. Therefore, your responsibility during a meeting is much greater than simply presenting a product.

A Life Insurance agent performs three important roles:

1. Listener
2. Analyst
3. Advisor

First Role: Listener

Before speaking, you must listen. Most agents make a mistake here. They start talking immediately after sitting. But a successful agent first understands the client's life.

Ask simple and friendly questions:

What work do you do?

How many family members depend on you?

Children studying in which class?

Do you have any loans?

What are your future plans for children?

When the client speaks, do not interrupt. Listening builds trust. The moment the customer feels you are interested in his life, his attitude towards you changes.

Second Role: Analyst

After listening carefully, mentally analyse the situation.

Check three important things:

- Income stability
- Number of dependents
- Future responsibilities

This helps you understand how much protection is actually required. Every customer does not need the same plan. A bachelor, a married person, and a parent require different types of planning.

Insurance should be recommended based on need, not convenience.

Third Role: Advisor

Only after understanding the situation should you recommend a solution.

Now you can explain:

"If something happens to the earning member, this much monthly amount should reach the family."

Explain in simple language. Avoid technical words. Customers understand life examples better than calculations.

Instead of saying "sum assured," say "family protection amount."

Instead of saying "policy term," say "years of family safety."

Instead of saying "premium," say "monthly security savings."

The customer should feel you are solving their problem, not selling your product.

The Correct Meeting Structure

Every successful Life Insurance meeting follows a simple order:

1. Greeting and comfort conversation
2. Family discussion
3. Need creation
4. Solution suggestion
5. Plan explanation
6. Closing decision

Most agents start directly at Step 5. Successful agents spend more time on Steps 2 and 3.

When the need becomes clear, the policy becomes easy.

Important Rule

Never start a meeting with a file.

Start with a conversation.

Files create distance. Conversations create connection.

Body Language Matters

Sit comfortably, maintain a pleasant smile, and keep a calm tone. Do not appear in a hurry. A relaxed agent gives confidence to the client. A tense agent creates doubt.

Avoid arguments. If a customer disagrees, listen respectfully and respond politely. Remember, you are building a relationship, not winning a debate.

End of Meeting

Even if the customer does not immediately decide, end positively:

"Thank you for your time. Think peacefully with your family. I will meet you again."

This leaves a good impression and increases the chance of future acceptance.

A good Life Insurance agent does not try to impress the customer.

He tries to understand the customer.

Understanding leads to trust.

Trust leads to a decision.

Decision leads to policy.

Your success in Life Insurance does not depend on how much you speak.

It depends on how well you understand people.

When you act as a guide instead of a seller, customers will not avoid you — they will wait for you.

CHAPTER 04

WHY PEOPLE AVOID INSURANCE AGENTS

Many Life Insurance agents experience a common problem. The moment people see them, they say, "I am busy," "I will call later," or "Not interested." Some even avoid phone calls. This hurts the confidence of agents, and they start believing customers do not like insurance.

The truth is different.

Customers do not avoid insurance.

Customers avoid uncomfortable experiences.

If we honestly observe, people happily buy mobile phones, vehicles, and even expensive items. Then why do they hesitate only for insurance? The answer is not the product. The answer is the approach.

Several common mistakes make customers uncomfortable.

1. Talking Only About Policy

Many agents start the conversation directly with plans, tables, and premium amounts. Within the first minute, the customer understands the purpose of the visit and mentally closes the discussion. A person first wants to feel comfortable, not pressured.

People like conversation before commitment.

When an agent starts with human interaction instead of policy explanation, the customer relaxes. A few minutes of genuine conversation can open a door that a long explanation cannot.

2. Creating Pressure

Statements like "Today is the last date," "Offer closing," or repeated phone calls create resistance. Customers may buy products under pressure once, but they never build long-term relationships. Insurance is a long-term commitment, so the decision must be peaceful.

A pressured customer becomes a lost customer.

Guide the customer, but never push the customer.

3. Lack of Listening

Some agents speak continuously without allowing the client to express their thoughts. When customers feel unheard, they lose interest. People trust those who listen to them patiently.

Listening is more powerful than explaining.

4. Contact Only for Business

If an agent calls only when he needs a policy, the customer feels used. But when an agent calls occasionally just to greet on birthdays, festivals, or policy reminders, the relationship becomes personal.

Relationship creates receptiveness.

5. Overpromising

Promising unrealistic returns or giving incorrect information creates serious damage. One negative experience spreads quickly to relatives and friends. Trust once broken is very difficult to rebuild.

In insurance, honesty is not only ethics — it is a business strategy.

6. Poor Follow-Up Method

Two extreme mistakes happen. Either the agent never follows up, or he follows up too aggressively. Both are harmful. Proper follow-up means polite reminders at reasonable intervals, not daily disturbance.

A gentle reminder keeps the connection alive.

7. Focusing Only on Money

When an agent talks only about maturity amount and returns, customers compare it with other investments. Then insurance becomes just another financial product. The true value of insurance — protection — is lost.

Insurance should first be explained as safety, not as profit.

Correct Approach

- First, build comfort.
- Then build trust.
- Then create a need.
- Finally, suggest a solution.

When the customer feels you care about his family, he will not avoid you. In fact, he will invite you again.

Remember an important principle:

People don't like being sold.

People like being guided.

Your behaviour decides your acceptance.

If you become a person who gives awareness instead of pressure, customers will welcome you. The same people who once avoided you will later recommend you to others.

The profession does not create rejection.

The approach creates rejection.

Change the approach, and the response will change.

CHAPTER 05

BUILDING THE RIGHT MINDSET FOR SUCCESS

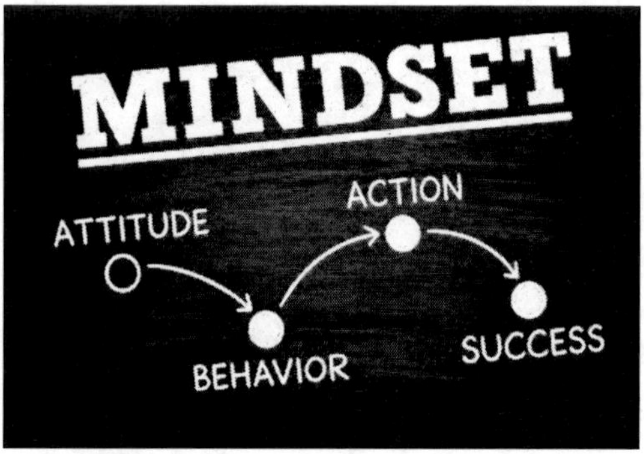

In the Life Insurance profession, product knowledge is important, but mindset is more important. Two agents may work in the same area, with the same plans and opportunities, yet one becomes successful while the other struggles. The difference is not intelligence or contacts. The difference is thinking.

Success in insurance begins in the mind before it appears in the field.

Many new agents enter the profession with enthusiasm but quickly lose confidence after hearing a few rejections. They start thinking, "People are not interested," "Market is bad," or "This profession is difficult." Slowly, hesitation increases, activity decreases, and performance stops.

Rejection is not the end of this profession. It is the training of this profession.

Every "no" you hear is not a personal insult. It is simply a person postponing a decision. Most customers reject not because they dislike you, but because they have not yet understood the importance of protection.

A successful agent thinks differently. Instead of feeling discouraged, he asks himself, "How can I explain better next time?" This small change in attitude keeps him moving forward.

Remove Three Fears

Three major fears stop agents from performing:

1. Fear of approaching people
2. Fear of rejection
3. Fear of what others think

The solution is simple — activity. Confidence does not come before action. Confidence comes after repeated action. The more people you meet, the more comfortable you become.

No agent becomes confident by waiting at home.

Self-Image Matters

If you think, "I am only an insurance agent," your voice becomes weak and hesitant. But if you think, "I am helping families secure their future," your communication automatically becomes strong and natural.

Your belief about yourself becomes visible in your behaviour.

Stand straight, speak clearly, and introduce yourself proudly. When you respect your profession, others will respect you.

Positive Routine

Start your day positively. Read something motivational, review your goals, and plan your activities. Avoid beginning the day with negative news or complaints. A positive morning creates a productive day.

Create a simple daily rule:

Meet people every day, regardless of mood.

Mood should not control activity. Activity should control mood.

Handling Rejection

In this profession, rejection is normal. Even the most successful agents face refusals. The difference is that they do not stop.

Do not argue with customers. Thank them politely and move to the next prospect. Today's "not now" can become tomorrow's "yes" if you maintain a good relationship.

Remember:

Rejection closes a conversation, not an opportunity.

Goal and Discipline

Fix a clear target — not only an income target, but an activity target.

For example:

Number of calls per day.

Number of meetings per week.

When activity becomes regular, results become predictable.

Success in Life Insurance is not a miracle. It is a habit.

Surrounding Environment

Stay connected with positive people, senior agents, and mentors. Avoid spending time with those who continuously complain about market conditions. Negative discussion reduces energy and motivation.

Encouragement increases performance.

Patience and Consistency

Insurance is not a one-day success profession. The seeds you plant today will yield results after some time. Many agents quit just before their efforts begin to produce outcomes.

Consistency converts small efforts into big achievements.

Always remember:

This profession gives three rewards — income, respect, and satisfaction. But it gives them to those who continue with patience.

Believe in your work.

Believe in your service.

Believe in yourself.

When your belief becomes strong, your hesitation disappears, your communication improves, and your success naturally follows.

First belief, then action, then achievement.

Believe First — Achieve Next.

CHAPTER 06

CONFIDENCE DEVELOPMENT FOR FIELD WORK

Many Life Insurance agents know the plans very well, yet they hesitate when they meet a customer. Their voice becomes low, they forget what to say, and they quickly finish the meeting. The problem is not a lack of knowledge. The problem is a lack of confidence.

Confidence is not an inborn talent.

Confidence is a practised skill.

An agent becomes confident not by memorising plan details, but by improving preparation, behaviour, and communication.

1. Preparation Before Meeting

Confidence starts before the meeting, not during the meeting.

Before visiting a client, spend a few minutes preparing mentally. Know the person's name, occupation, and family details if possible. Decide the purpose of the visit and the first line you will speak. When your mind is clear, your speech becomes clear.

Never go to a customer with confusion. Preparation removes fear.

2. First Impression

The first two minutes decide the comfort level of the entire discussion.

Wear a neat and clean dress. You do not need expensive clothes, but you need a professional appearance. Maintain a pleasant smile. Greet respectfully and speak slowly. Avoid immediately opening your bag or file.

First create comfort, then create conversation.

People trust a person who appears organised and calm.

3. How to Start the Conversation

Do not start with policy discussion.

Begin with a friendly line:

"I came to discuss your future planning for family security."

This sounds caring instead of commercial. Speak naturally as if you are talking to a known person, not delivering a speech.

4. Voice and Speech

Speak clearly and at a moderate speed. A very fast voice shows nervousness, and a very slow voice shows a lack of confidence. Maintain eye contact, but do not stare. Use simple words. Avoid technical terms in the beginning.

Your tone should be conversational, not promotional.

5. Body Language

Your body speaks before your words.

Sit straight but relaxed. Do not continuously look at papers. Keep your hands steady and avoid unnecessary movements. Nodding while listening shows respect and attention.

A calm body creates a confident image.

6. Handling Nervousness

Feeling nervous is normal, especially in the early stages. Instead of avoiding meetings, increase meetings. Practice reduces tension. After several discussions, speaking becomes natural.

Remember:

You are not facing an examiner.

You are talking to a person who also has worries about his family's future.

Think of yourself as a helper, not a seller. Nervousness will reduce automatically.

7. What to Do If You Forget

Sometimes you may forget a point during a discussion. Do not panic. Pause, smile, and continue with another question. Customers do not expect perfection. They expect sincerity.

Confidence is not speaking without mistakes.

Confidence is continuing without fear.

8. Ending the Meeting

Do not rush to leave. Politely summarize:

"We discussed family protection and children's future planning. Please think with your family. I will meet you again."

A calm ending leaves a positive impression.

Practice Method

Every day, practice speaking for a few minutes in front of a mirror. Introduce yourself and explain the importance of family protection. This simple exercise greatly improves fluency and self-belief.

Important Truth

Customers do not judge you by how many plans you know.

They judge you by how comfortable they feel with you.

When comfort increases, trust increases.

When trust increases, decisions become easy.

Confidence grows step by step. Each meeting improves your ability. Do not wait to become confident before starting. Start working, and confidence will come.

Your confidence gives confidence to the customer.

And a confident agent always creates a confident decision.

CHAPTER 07

THE PSYCHOLOGY OF CUSTOMERS

Many Life Insurance agents believe customers refuse because they do not have money. In reality, most refusals do not come from financial problems. They come from human thinking patterns.

Insurance is not a mathematical decision.

Insurance is a psychological decision.

To succeed in this profession, an agent must understand how people think, feel, and decide.

1. People Avoid Unpleasant Thoughts

Life insurance reminds a person about risk, illness, and death. Naturally, people do not like to think about such topics. Therefore, when an agent starts directly with "insurance policy," the customer's mind immediately resists the conversation.

It is not a rejection of you.

It is avoidance of an uncomfortable topic.

Instead of speaking about death, speak about responsibility, children's future, and family stability. The mind accepts positive protection more easily than negative fear.

2. People Delay Important Decisions

Human nature prefers urgent pleasures over important planning. Buying a phone, vehicle, or clothing gives immediate satisfaction. Insurance gives long-term security, which is invisible today. Because there is no immediate reward, people postpone.

This is called postponement behaviour.

Your role is to gently move the customer from postponement to planning by helping him imagine future situations.

3. Emotional Decision First, Logical Decision Later

Customers think they decide logically, but most decisions begin emotionally. A father decides after imagining his children's future. A mother agrees after thinking about family safety.

First, the heart agrees.

Then the mind justifies.

Therefore, examples and life situations are more powerful than complex calculations.

4. Trust Before Product

Before accepting your plan, the customer evaluates you. He observes your honesty, patience, and behaviour. If trust is built, even a simple explanation is enough. Without trust, even the best plan fails.

Customers buy the advisor first, and the policy next.

5. Fear of Loss Is Stronger Than Desire for Gain

People may not act to earn extra returns, but they act quickly to avoid loss. When a person understands the financial difficulty his family may face in his absence, seriousness increases.

Protection motivates faster than profit.

However, this should be explained sensitively, not by frightening the customer, but by helping him realise responsibility.

6. Social Proof

Many people decide based on what others are doing. When you mention that similar families or friends have planned their protection, confidence increases.

People feel safer following a proven path.

7. The Need for Simplicity

Too many numbers, tables, and technical terms create confusion. A confused mind postpones decisions. A clear and simple explanation encourages decisions.

Confusion creates delay.

Clarity creates action.

8. Respect and Recognition

Customers like to feel important. Listen patiently, appreciate their responsibilities, and respect their opinions. When they feel valued, they become cooperative.

People remember how you made them feel more than what you explained.

Practical Principle

Do not try to defeat the customer's logic.

Guide the customer's thinking.

Ask thoughtful questions, let them express concerns, and help them reach their own conclusion. When customers feel the decision is theirs, acceptance becomes strong and lasting.

Understanding psychology changes your approach. You stop forcing and start guiding. You stop explaining too much and start asking the right questions.

A successful Life Insurance agent is not the one who speaks the most.

He is the one who understands the mind of the customer the best.

When you understand people, selling becomes serving.

And serving creates success naturally.

CHAPTER 08

FIRST IMPRESSION AND PERSONAL GROOMING

In the Life Insurance profession, customers decide their comfort level within the first few seconds of meeting you. Before you explain a plan, before you ask a question, and even before you sit down, your appearance and behaviour already communicate a message.

First impressions speak faster than words.

A customer may not know your knowledge, but he immediately notices your personality. A neat and professional appearance builds confidence, while a careless appearance creates doubt.

You do not need costly clothes or luxury accessories. You need cleanliness, simplicity, and professionalism.

1. Dress Code

Wear clean, well-ironed clothes. A simple formal shirt and trousers are sufficient. Shoes should be polished and neat. Avoid very bright or distracting colours. Soft and decent colours create a trustworthy look.

Your dressing should make the customer feel, “This person is serious about his work.”

2. Personal Hygiene

Maintain basic grooming habits:

- Clean hair
- Trimmed nails
- Fresh breath
- Neat shave or properly maintained beard

These small details greatly influence comfort. Customers may not comment on them, but they definitely notice them.

3. Carrying Materials

Carry a neat folder or an organised bag. Papers should be arranged properly. Avoid searching for documents during discussion. When you appear organised, customers assume your work is also organised.

An organisation increases credibility.

4. Greeting Etiquette

Greet politely with a smile. Use respectful words. Speak the customer's name correctly. A warm greeting immediately reduces distance.

A smile is the simplest and most powerful communication tool.

5. Sitting Behaviour

Sit only after being invited. Sit straight but relaxed. Do not lean too much forward or backwards. Keep your mobile phone silent and avoid checking it during the discussion. This shows respect.

Attention shows importance.

6. Body Language

Maintain natural eye contact while speaking. Do not cross arms defensively. Keep gentle hand movements while explaining. Nodding while listening shows involvement and understanding.

Your body language should communicate confidence and calmness.

7. Punctuality

Arrive on time. If delayed, inform the customer in advance. Respecting time shows professionalism. A punctual agent is trusted more than a knowledgeable but careless agent.

Time respect builds relationship respect.

8. Positive Attitude

Enter the meeting with positive energy. Do not carry previous rejection into the next meeting. Every customer is a new opportunity.

Customers can feel your attitude even if you do not speak about it.

Important Truth

People form opinions quickly and change them slowly. A good first impression makes your explanation easier. A poor first impression makes your task difficult, even if your plan is excellent.

Therefore, before improving your presentation, improve your presence.

Your appearance opens the door.

Your behaviour keeps the door open.

Your guidance completes the work.

Professional grooming is not about showing status.

It is about showing respect — respect for the customer, respect for the profession, and respect for yourself.

When you look professional, you feel confident.

When you feel confident, you speak clearly.

When you speak clearly, customers trust you.

And trust is the beginning of every policy.

CHAPTER 09

HOW TO APPROACH A NEW CUSTOMER

For many Life Insurance agents, the most difficult step is the first step — approaching a new person. They know the plans, they are ready to work, but hesitation stops them. They keep thinking, "What will he say?" or "What if he refuses?"

Remember one important truth:

The problem is not approaching people.

The problem is approaching them in the wrong way.

A stranger does not avoid you because you are a life insurance agent. He avoids you because he expects pressure. Your approach should remove pressure and create comfort.

1. Correct Mindset Before Approach

Do not go with the feeling, "I am going to sell a policy."

Go with the feeling, "I am going to discuss family planning and protection."

Your intention changes your communication. When your mind is relaxed, your conversation becomes natural.

2. Never Start with Policy

The biggest mistake agents make is introducing insurance in the first sentence. The moment the word "policy" is heard, the customer becomes defensive.

Instead, begin with a simple, polite introduction.

Example:

"Hello, sir, I am Sathya Prakash Urs. I work in family financial planning and protection services. I just wanted a few minutes to understand your future planning."

This line sounds advisory, not commercial.

3. Use Reference Approach

Approaching with a known reference increases acceptance.

"Your friend Mr Ramesh suggested I meet you regarding family financial security planning."

A reference creates immediate trust because the person feels you are not a random visitor.

4. Use Help-Based Approach

Instead of selling, offer help.

"I am meeting families in this area to help them review their children's education planning and retirement preparation."

People are more open to help than to sales.

5. Ask Simple Questions

After the introduction, do not start explaining. Ask questions:

- How many members are in your family?
- Children studying in which class?
- Any plans for higher education?

Questions involve the customer. A person who speaks becomes comfortable.

6. Avoid Long Speeches

Do not give a long explanation in the first meeting. The purpose of the first meeting is not to close the policy. The purpose is to open the relationship.

A short conversation today creates long business tomorrow.

7. If Customer Says Busy

Do not insist. Respectfully respond:

"I understand, sir. Please tell me a convenient time. I will meet you for just 10 minutes."

Respect increases the chance of a future appointment.

8. Ending the First Meeting

End positively:

"Thank you for your time. I will prepare a simple family protection suggestion and meet you again."

This creates curiosity and prepares for the next meeting.

Important Field Rule

First meeting = relationship

Second meeting = discussion

Third meeting = decision

Most agents try to finish everything in the first meeting and lose the opportunity.

Handling Fear

Approach more people. Fear reduces with repetition. The first 10 approaches feel difficult. The next 20 become easier. After 50, it becomes natural.

Action removes hesitation.

Golden Principle

People may refuse a policy.

They rarely refuse a polite and respectful person.

Therefore, focus on being friendly, patient, and sincere. When people feel comfortable with you, they will listen. When they listen, they will understand. When they understand, they will decide.

Your success in Life Insurance begins not with presentation, but with approach.

A good beginning creates a good ending.

CHAPTER 10

EFFECTIVE INTRODUCTION TECHNIQUES

The first few sentences you speak decide whether the customer will listen to you or try to finish the conversation quickly. Many Life Insurance agents lose opportunities not because of a lack of knowledge, but because of a weak introduction.

A strong introduction does not sell a policy.

A strong introduction opens a mind.

Your opening line should create comfort, curiosity, and respect — not pressure.

1. The Wrong Way

Avoid these types of openings:

"Sir, I came to explain a new policy."

"Sir, Life Insurance has a very good plan."

"Sir, just five minutes, I will show a table."

These sentences immediately alert the customer that a sales discussion is coming. The mind closes before the conversation begins.

2. The Correct Principle

Your introduction should focus on the customer's life, not your product.

Talk about:

- Family
- Future
- Responsibility
- Planning

When you talk about their life, they listen.

3. Powerful Opening Lines

You may use any of these:

"I am meeting families to discuss children's education security planning."

"I help earning members make sure their family does not face financial difficulty in their absence."

"I am not here to sell anything today. I just want to understand your current family protection planning."

"I guide parents on how to prepare funds for higher education and retirement safely."

These lines remove resistance because they sound helpful, not commercial.

4. Self-Introduction Method

Introduce yourself clearly and confidently:

"Good morning, sir. My name is Sathya Prakash Urs S N. I work in family financial protection and long-term security planning."

Speak slowly, smile, and maintain eye contact. Confidence in the introduction creates confidence in the discussion.

5. Use Question-Based Introduction

Questions engage the mind.

Example:

"Sir, may I ask one small question? If your income stops for a few months, will your family expenses continue comfortably?"

This question naturally leads to a meaningful discussion.

6. 30-Second Introduction Formula

Follow this simple order:

Greeting → Name → Purpose → Benefit.

Example:

"Good evening, sir. I am Sathya Prakash Urs S N. I work with families to ensure children's education and retirement income planning. I wanted to understand your current planning and see if any improvement is possible."

This takes less than 30 seconds but creates interest.

7. What to Avoid

- Do not speak too fast
- Do not apologise for meeting
- Do not appear nervous
- Do not immediately open your file

Your personality should introduce you before your papers do.

8. Practice Is Necessary

Practice your introduction daily in front of a mirror. Speak aloud until it becomes natural. When your opening becomes natural, your fear reduces.

Prepared words create natural confidence.

Important Reminder

Customers do not decide in the first minute.

They decide whether to continue listening in the first minute.

If your introduction is comfortable, they will give you time. Time creates understanding. Understanding creates a decision.

A good introduction is not a speech.

It is a respectful beginning of a relationship.

And every successful policy begins with a successful introduction.

CHAPTER 11

BUILDING TRUST BEFORE BUSINESS

In the Life Insurance profession, customers rarely decide based only on the plan. They decide based on the person who explains the plan. If trust is strong, even a simple explanation is enough. Without trust, even the best plan will be rejected.

People do not buy policies.

People buy confidence.

Many agents try to close business quickly. They immediately start explaining tables, returns, and benefits. But the customer is not yet ready. Before accepting your advice, the customer silently asks himself one question:

“Can I trust this person?”

Your first responsibility is not selling a policy.

Your first responsibility is earning trust.

1. Give Time Before Expecting a Decision

Trust does not develop in a hurry. Spend a few minutes in general conversation. Ask about the customer’s work, family, and daily routine. Do not rush into business discussion.

When a person feels comfortable, their mind opens. When the mind opens, he listens.

2. Listen More, Speak Less

Allow the customer to talk about his life and responsibilities. Listen carefully without interrupting. When you listen sincerely, the customer feels respected.

Respect creates connection.

Most people are not heard patiently in daily life. When you listen attentively, you become different from others.

3. Show Genuine Interest

Remember small details: children’s names, exams, job changes, or health issues. Mention them in future meetings.

For example:

“How is your son’s college preparation going?”

This simple line creates a strong personal bond.

4. Be Honest and Clear

Never promise unrealistic returns. Never hide conditions. If a plan has limitations, explain them clearly. A customer may postpone a decision, but he will not lose respect for honesty.

Honesty may delay one policy.

Dishonesty may destroy many policies.

Trust grows slowly but breaks quickly.

5. Do Not Argue

If a customer disagrees or compares with another investment, do not argue. Calmly explain your point and respect his opinion.

Winning an argument may lose a relationship.

Losing an argument may win a customer.

6. Service After Policy

Real trust begins after policy issuance. Many agents disappear after receiving commission. Instead, maintain contact.

- Remind premium dates
- Help with address changes
- Assist in nomination updates
- Help during claim procedures

When the customer sees your support after business hours, their confidence becomes permanent.

7. Be Consistent

Your behaviour should be the same in every meeting. Politeness only during the sale and indifference later reduces credibility. Consistency builds reliability.

Reliability builds reputation.

8. Keep Your Word

If you promise to call, call.

If you promise to visit, visit.

Small commitments build big trust.

Important Understanding

Trust is not created by impressive speaking.

Trust is created by dependable behaviour.

When customers trust you, they stop comparing plans. They stop delaying decisions. They also refer their relatives and friends willingly.

A trusted agent does not search for customers.

Customers search for the trusted agent.

Always remember:

Before asking for a signature, earn belief.

Before explaining a policy, build a relationship.

Business built on pressure ends quickly.

A business built on trust continues for years.

Trust first — business next.

This is the permanent success formula in Life Insurance.

CHAPTER 12

CREATING THE NEED FOR INSURANCE

Many Life Insurance agents explain plans very well, yet customers say, "I will think later." The real reason is simple — the customer has understood the plan, but he has not felt the need.

People do not buy insurance because it is available.

People buy insurance because it becomes necessary in their minds.

Your most important skill is not explaining benefits.

Your most important skill is helping the customer realise responsibility.

1. Do Not Start with the Plan

The biggest mistake is opening the file and showing tables immediately. A person who has not realised the need will only see premium as an expense.

First, create a need.

Then present the solution.

Insurance should appear as an answer, not as an offer.

2. Use Questions to Create Thinking

Never lecture. Ask simple questions that make the customer think:

- "If income stops for some months, how will family expenses continue?"
- "Have you planned funds for your children's higher education?"
- "If retirement comes tomorrow, what will be your monthly income source?"
- "Do you have a financial backup for emergencies?"

Questions activate the mind. When a person answers himself, realisation becomes stronger.

3. Responsibility Discussion

Gently discuss responsibilities:

- Family monthly expenses
- Children's education
- Marriage expenses

- Outstanding loans
- Old age security

Help the customer calculate approximately how much money the family needs every month. When he realises the amount, the seriousness increases.

Awareness creates urgency.

4. Use Life Situations

Explain practical situations instead of technical points.

"Suppose an earning member is not present tomorrow. Rent, school fees, groceries — all continue. The family needs regular income support. That support should be planned today."

Do not frighten. Do not exaggerate. Speak calmly and realistically.

5. The Protection Gap

Help the customer understand the difference between current savings and the actual requirement.

Many people have savings, but savings may not be sufficient for long-term security. When the customer sees the gap, the need becomes clear.

Clarity leads to acceptance.

6. Emotional Connection

Insurance is connected with love and responsibility. When a parent thinks about their children's future, the decision becomes easier.

People may ignore their own comfort.

They rarely ignore their family's safety.

7. Only After Need — Present the Plan

Now introduce the plan as a solution:

"This plan ensures that your family receives financial support even if income stops."

At this stage, the customer does not see premium as a burden. He sees it as protection.

8. Avoid Forcing

If the customer needs time, allow him. Realisation continues even after the meeting. A peaceful decision becomes a lasting policy.

Pressure creates resistance.

Understanding creates acceptance.

Golden Rule

When the need is weak, explanation becomes difficult.

When the need is strong, explanation becomes simple.

Your job is not to convince forcefully.

Your job is to guide thoughtfully.

A policy is not closed by talking more.

A policy is closed when the customer understands more.

Therefore remember:

Create awareness → Create need → Provide solution.

When a customer feels, "This is important for my family," the decision naturally follows.

Need creates a decision.

Decision creates policy.

Policy creates protection.

CHAPTER 13

EMOTIONAL VS LOGICAL DECISION MAKING

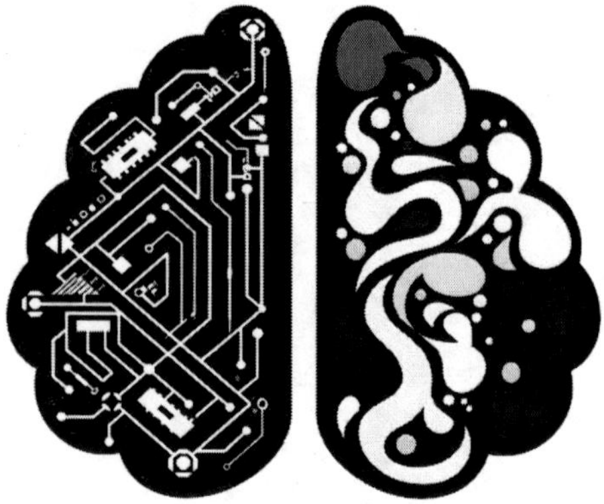

Many Life Insurance agents experience a confusing situation. The customer listens carefully, agrees with your points, appreciates your explanation, and even says, "You explained very well." Yet at the end, he says, "I will think and tell you later."

The agent feels surprised.

"If he understood everything, why did he not decide?"

Because the decision was logical, but not yet emotional.

Human decisions do not happen only in the mind. They happen in two stages — first in the heart, then in the brain.

Emotion creates intention.

Logic creates justification.

If only logic is present, the customer postpones. If emotion is present, the customer decides.

1. Logical Thinking

Logical thinking includes calculations:

- Premium amount
- Bonus
- Maturity value
- Returns

These points help the customer understand the plan, but they do not always create urgency. The customer may say, “I will plan later when convenient.”

Logic informs.

Emotion motivates.

2. Emotional Thinking

Emotional thinking connects with responsibility:

- Children’s future
- Spouse security
- Parents’ support
- Peace of mind

When a person imagines his family depending on him, seriousness increases. This does not mean frightening the customer. It means helping him visualise responsibility.

For example:

"If something unexpected interrupts your income, your family should continue their lifestyle without difficulty. Planning today gives them that confidence."

This connects emotionally without creating fear.

3. Why Customers Delay

Delay happens when logic is clear, but emotion is weak. The customer understands the plan but does not feel urgency.

Insurance competes with comfort. Comfort is immediate; security is future. Without emotional realisation, the customer chooses comfort and postpones security.

4. Correct Balance

Do not depend only on emotional stories. Also, do not depend only on calculations. Use both.

First, help the customer feel the importance.

Then help the customer understand the solution.

Emotion opens the mind.

Logic confirms the decision.

5. Family Discussion

Encourage the customer to discuss with their spouse. Often, the final decision becomes stronger when the family understands the purpose.

A joint understanding becomes a permanent commitment.

6. Peaceful Closing

After explanation, calmly summarise:

"We discussed your family protection and future responsibilities. This plan ensures continuity even if income stops. Please make a comfortable decision."

Do not rush. Silence for a few seconds is powerful. Give the customer time to think.

7. Important Understanding

Customers rarely regret buying protection.

They often regret postponing protection.

Your role is to help them avoid future regret.

Key Principle

People invest for growth.

People insure for care.

When customers feel you care about their family, their emotional confidence increases. Logical questions reduce naturally.

A successful agent does not push decisions.

He helps decisions happen naturally.

When heart agrees and mind understands, signature follows.

Insurance is not sold by pressure.

It is accepted by realization.

CHAPTER 14

ASKING POWERFUL QUESTIONS

In the Life Insurance profession, many agents believe success depends on how well they explain. In reality, success depends on how well they ask.

Good agents talk well. Great agents ask well.

When you continuously explain, the customer listens politely but remains passive. When you ask meaningful questions, the customer starts thinking and participating. A thinking customer becomes a deciding customer.

Questions are powerful because the answers come from the customer themselves. A person trusts his own conclusion more than someone else's explanation.

1. Purpose of Asking Questions

Questions help you:

- Understand the customer's situation
- Build involvement
- Create awareness
- Develop needs naturally

Never ask questions like an interrogation. Ask gently, like in a conversation.

2. Family Responsibility Questions

These questions create seriousness:

"How many people depend on your income?"

"What are your plans for your children's higher education?"

"If your income pauses for a few months, how will expenses continue?"

"Do you have a separate fund only for family security?"

These questions help the customer realise his responsibilities.

3. Financial Planning Questions

"Do you currently have a regular monthly savings habit?"

"Is your savings meant for investment or protection?"

"Have you planned a guaranteed income after retirement?"

"Are your current savings sufficient for long-term family needs?"

The customer begins to evaluate his own planning.

4. Risk Awareness Questions

"Have you calculated how much money your family would require monthly in your absence?" "If a medical or financial emergency happens, which fund will you use first?"

"Is there any arrangement that continues income for your family automatically?"

These questions create awareness without frightening the customer.

5. Decision-Making Questions

After discussion, ask gently:

"Do you feel family protection planning is necessary?"

"Would you prefer monthly savings or yearly savings?"

"When would you like this protection to start?"

These questions guide the customer toward action.

6. Rules for Asking Questions

- Ask one question at a time
- Listen fully to the answer
- Do not interrupt
- Appreciate the response

Listening after asking is more important than asking itself.

7. Avoid Wrong Questions

Do not ask:

"Will you take policy?"

"Are you ready now?"

These questions create pressure and resistance.

Instead, ask guiding questions that help the customer reach the decision themselves.

8. The Power of Silence

After an important question, pause. Silence allows thinking. Many agents speak again too quickly and reduce the effect of the question.

A thoughtful pause is a part of communication.

Important Understanding

Explaining forces attention.

Questioning creates realisation.

When a customer realises the need himself, he does not feel convinced — he feels convinced by his own thinking.

And decisions made by self-realisation rarely cancel later.

Therefore remember:

Talk less.

Ask more.

Listen deeply.

The right question at the right time is stronger than the longest explanation.

Questions open minds.

Open minds accept decisions.

CHAPTER 15

UNDERSTANDING FAMILY RESPONSIBILITIES

Life insurance is not really about money.

It is about responsibility.

Every earning person carries invisible responsibilities on their shoulders. He works daily not only for his present needs but also for the safety and stability of his family. When a life insurance agent understands these responsibilities, the conversation becomes meaningful instead of commercial.

Do not first see the customer as a client.

First, see him as a parent, spouse, or son.

1. The Earning Member's Role

In most families, one person's income supports many lives. Monthly expenses, school fees, groceries, medical needs, and future plans all depend on that income. If that income suddenly stops, the entire family's routine is disturbed.

Expenses never stop.

Only income can stop.

Helping the earning member realise this is not frightening him; it is helping him plan wisely.

2. Children's Education

Every parent wants the best education for their children. But education costs increase every year. Higher studies, professional courses, and skill training require long-term financial preparation.

Ask gently:

"If your child reaches college age tomorrow, is the fund already prepared?"

When a parent thinks about education, seriousness naturally increases. Parents may compromise on personal comfort, but rarely on their children's future.

Education planning creates strong acceptance for long-term protection.

3. Family Monthly Expenses

Families depend on regular income. Rent or loan, electricity, food, transport — these continue every month. Savings alone may not support these expenses for a long period.

Explain calmly:

"The family needs not only a lump sum amount, but also continuity of financial support."

This helps the customer understand the importance of adequate coverage.

4. Loan and Liabilities

Many families have housing loans, personal loans, or other commitments. If the earning member is not present, the burden shifts to the family. This can create emotional and financial stress.

Protection planning ensures that liabilities do not become a lifelong problem for the family.

5. Responsibility Toward Parents

In many homes, elderly parents depend on their children for support. Medical expenses and daily needs require stability. A well-planned protection ensures dignity for parents even in difficult times.

Security preserves self-respect.

6. Retirement Responsibility

One day, income will stop naturally — retirement. After retirement, expenses continue, but earning capacity reduces. Without planning, a person may become dependent on others.

Retirement planning is not about wealth.

It is about independence.

7. Connecting Responsibility to Solution

After discussing responsibilities, gently explain:

"All these responsibilities can be protected with proper planning started today."

Now the customer sees insurance not as an expense, but as a safeguard.

Important Understanding

People do not buy insurance for documents or tax benefits.

They buy it for people they love.

When you connect the discussion to family care instead of a financial product, the decision becomes emotional and meaningful.

Agent's True Role

You are not reminding a person about risk.

You are reminding him of his responsibility.

Responsibility creates seriousness.

Seriousness creates action.

Action creates protection.

Every policy you complete is not just business.

It is a promise that a family will not suffer financially.

And that is the real purpose of this profession.

CHAPTER 16

PRESENTING LIFE INSURANCE AS PROTECTION

One common mistake many Life Insurance agents make is presenting insurance as an investment. They talk mainly about bonuses, returns, and maturity amount. When insurance is explained only this way, customers compare it with other financial products and start calculating profits.

Insurance should not be introduced as a profit plan.

Insurance should be introduced as a protection plan.

The primary purpose of life insurance is security. Returns are secondary benefits. When the customer understands this correctly, objections reduce naturally.

1. Change the Explanation Method

Instead of saying:

"This policy will give maturity after 20 years."

Explain like this:

"This arrangement ensures your family receives financial support even if your income stops."

The second sentence gives meaning, not just information.

2. Use Simple Language

Avoid technical words such as sum assured, survival benefit, and term period in the beginning. Use simple, everyday language:

- Family protection amount
- Safety period
- Guaranteed support
- Future security fund

When the customer understands easily, confidence increases.

3. Explain the Real Value

Tell the customer:

"We insure house, vehicle, and mobile because they are valuable. But the most valuable asset is your income.

Life insurance protects the income that supports your family."

This helps the customer see insurance logically and emotionally.

4. Monthly Example Method

People understand monthly expenses better than large numbers.

Example:

"If your family needs ₹30,000 per month, they need continuous support. This plan ensures financial stability for them even in your absence."

Practical examples create clarity.

5. Protection First, Benefit Next

Follow this order while explaining:

First — Why is protection necessary.

Second — How the plan gives protection.

Third — What additional benefits come later.

If you reverse the order, the customer only focuses on returns.

6. Avoid Over-Explanation

Do not overload with details. Too much information creates confusion. Give essential points clearly. Answer additional questions when asked.

Clarity is stronger than complexity.

7. Use Visual Imagination

Help the customer imagine:

"Your family continues their lifestyle, children continue their education, and responsibilities are managed smoothly because planning was done earlier."

When customers visualise security, they value the plan more.

8. Close With Assurance

End explanation with confidence:

"This is not only a saving. This is a financial safety arrangement for your family."

Important Truth

Investment plans grow money.

Insurance plans protect life.

When you present insurance as protection, the customer stops comparing and starts appreciating.

Your role is not to impress with calculations.

Your role is to create understanding.

Once the customer understands protection, acceptance becomes easy.

Protection gives peace of mind.

Peace of mind creates a decision.

Decision creates policy.

And that policy becomes a shield for the family's future.

CHAPTER 17

EXPLAINING PLANS IN SIMPLE LANGUAGE

Many Life Insurance agents know every detail of the plan, yet customers remain confused. The reason is not lack of knowledge. The reason is complicated explanation.

Customers do not reject insurance because it is costly.

They reject it because it is confusing.

A confused mind postpones decisions. A clear mind accepts decisions.

Your goal is not to show how much you know.

Your goal is to help the customer understand easily.

1. Avoid Technical Terms

When you use technical words like *sum assured, survival benefit, maturity value, policy term*, customers feel the discussion is complicated. They hesitate to ask questions and silently delay the decision.

Instead, convert technical words into simple meanings:

Sum Assured → Family protection amount.

Policy Term → Years of safety.

Premium → Monthly savings for family security.

Maturity → Future guaranteed fund.

Simple words create confidence.

2. The Three-Sentence Method

Explain any plan in just three simple points:

1. What you pay
2. What protection do you get
3. What benefit comes later

Example:

"You save a small amount regularly. During the protection period, your family is financially secured. After completion, you also receive a future fund."

This is easier to understand than a long presentation.

3. Do Not Start with Numbers

Numbers create comparison. Meaning creates interest.

First, explain the purpose, then explain the amount.

Wrong way:

"This is a 20-year policy with this premium and this return."

Correct way:

"This is a long-term family safety arrangement. The saving amount is small and comfortable, and it guarantees protection throughout the period."

4. Use Everyday Examples

Compare with common life situations:

"We lock our home before leaving because we care about safety. This plan locks your family's financial safety."

Simple comparisons make ideas memorable.

5. Encourage Questions

"Is my explanation clear?"

"Would you like me to explain again in a simpler way?"

When customers feel free to ask, they become relaxed and involved.

6. Speak Slowly and Clearly

Many agents speak fast due to nervousness. Speak slowly with small pauses. Give time for understanding.

Understanding is more important than speed.

7. Summarise at the End

Before finishing, repeat briefly:

"This plan gives you protection during the period and a future fund afterwards."

Repetition strengthens clarity.

8. One Important Rule

Do not try to explain every feature. Explain only what is useful for the customer's need. Too much information creates doubt.

The right information at the right time creates confidence.

Key Understanding

Customers may forget numbers.

They remember meaning.

When they clearly understand the benefit to their family, they will not worry about complexity.

Your words should remove confusion, not increase it.

Simple explanation → Clear understanding → Confident decision.

A good agent does not give the longest presentation.

A good agent is one whose explanation is easiest to understand.

When the customer says, "Now I understand," you are close to a policy.

Clarity closes more policies than cleverness.

CHAPTER 18

BENEFITS VS FEATURES — WHAT CUSTOMERS UNDERSTAND

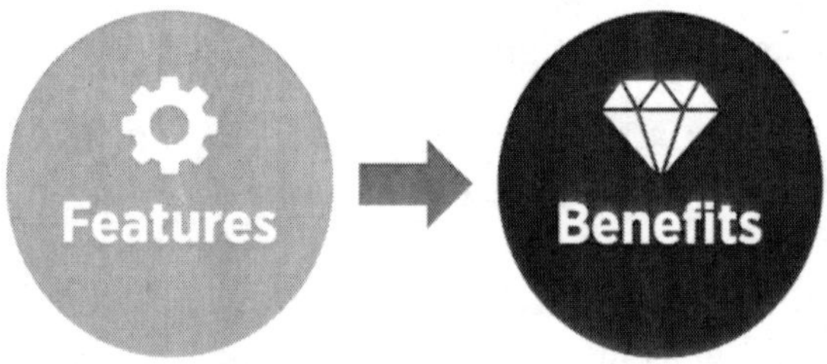

A common mistake in the Life Insurance profession is over-explaining plan features. Agents speak about the term, bonus rate, table number, and conditions for many minutes. The customer listens politely but does not feel motivated to decide.

Because customers do not buy features.

Customers buy benefits.

A feature is a technical description of the plan.

A benefit is the practical advantage to the customer's life.

Features inform the mind.

Benefits convince the heart.

1. Understanding the Difference

Feature:

"This is a 20-year endowment policy."

Benefit:

"Your family remains financially secure for the next 20 years."

Feature:

"There is a maturity amount with a bonus."

Benefit:

"You receive a guaranteed fund when your child reaches higher education age."

Feature:

"There is a risk cover."

Benefit:

"Even if income stops, your family will continue their lifestyle."

The same plan sounds completely different when explained as a benefit.

2. Why Benefits Work

Customers are not interested in insurance terminology. They are interested in how their problems are solved. When they hear benefits, they connect the plan with their own life.

People listen to what matters to them.

3. Convert Every Feature into Benefit

Before meeting a client, prepare simple benefit statements:

Instead of saying premium amount, say comfortable monthly savings.

Instead of saying coverage period, say years of family protection.

Instead of saying claim amount, say financial support for family.

When the customer hears a life-related meaning, attention increases.

4. Focus on Personal Relevance

Explain the benefits according to the customer's situation.

For a parent:

"This ensures your child's education continues without interruption."

For a salaried person:

"This replaces your income support for your family."

For a middle-aged person:

"This prepares a secure fund for retirement."

Personal relevance creates importance.

5. Avoid Information Overload

Too many details reduce interest. Give only the information needed to understand the benefit. Additional details can be provided later if required.

Simplicity increases acceptance.

6. Emotional Connection

Benefits create emotional comfort. When customers imagine their family safe and secure, hesitation reduces.

Emotion strengthens a decision.

7. Final Summary Method

Always conclude by restating the main benefit:

"This plan protects your family now and supports your future later."

A clear final message stays in the customer's mind even after you leave.

Important Principle

A customer may not remember policy details.

He remembers how the plan helps his family.

When customers clearly see the benefit, the premium appears reasonable. When they see only features, the premium appears expensive.

Therefore:

Do not present policies.

Present protection.

Do not describe plans.

Describe security.

Features explain the product.

Benefits explain the purpose.

And the purpose is what makes the customer decide.

CHAPTER 19

HANDLING COMMON OBJECTIONS

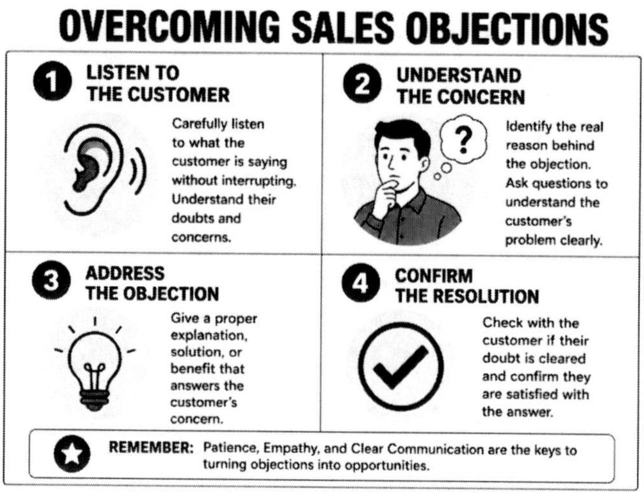

In the Life Insurance profession, objections are normal. They are not rejected. They are questions in another form.

When a customer gives an objection, he is not saying "no."

He is saying, "I need more clarity."

A confident agent does not fear objections. He understands them and responds patiently.

Rule Number One:

Never argue. Never react emotionally. Always respond calmly.

Your tone should be friendly, not defensive.

1. **"I will think and tell later."**

This is the most common response. Usually, it means the customer has not yet realised urgency.

Reply gently:

"Certainly, sir, it is an important decision. May I ask which part you would like to think about — the amount or the timing? I can clarify if needed."

This helps the customer express the real concern.

2. **"I don't have money now."**

Do not immediately reduce the plan or leave.

Respond:

"I understand. Protection should always be comfortable. That is why we plan a small regular saving instead of a large amount later. Even a small start today is better than a big start tomorrow."

Then offer a suitable, smaller option.

3. **"Already I have policies."**

Appreciate first.

"That is very good. It shows you care about your family."

Then continue:

"May I ask — is your current coverage sufficient for your present responsibilities? As income and family grow, protection also needs review."

This converts the objection into a discussion.

4. "I will invest somewhere else."

Do not criticise other investments.

Respond calmly:

"Investments are for growth. Insurance is for safety. Both are important. This arrangement ensures your family is secure while your other investments grow peacefully."

You position insurance differently instead of competing.

5. "My friend is also an agent."

Respect the relationship.

"That is good. It is always nice to have trusted guidance. You may continue with him. My purpose is only to ensure your protection is adequate. If you ever need assistance or clarification, I am always available."

Respect builds goodwill and sometimes future business.

6. "I am young. I will plan later."

Explain the timing benefit.

"That is exactly why planning is easier now. Younger age means lower cost and longer protection. Waiting increases cost but not security."

Help them see the advantage of early action.

7. "Send details on WhatsApp."

Do not depend only on messages.

"Sure, I will send a brief summary. But this planning needs a short discussion as it relates to your family. When would be a convenient time for us to meet for 10 minutes?"

Bring the conversation back to a meeting.

Important Techniques

- Listen fully before replying
- Acknowledge the concern
- Answer simply
- Ask a follow-up question

Objections handled patiently often become acceptance.

Golden Understanding

An uninterested person avoids discussion.

A questioning person is a potential customer.

Therefore, welcome objections. They mean the customer is thinking seriously.

Stay calm, stay respectful, and stay helpful.

Every objection is not a barrier.

It is a step closer to clarity.

Clarity leads to confidence.

Confidence leads to a decision.

And the decision leads to policy.

CHAPTER 20

DEALING WITH "I WILL THINK LATER" CUSTOMERS

"I will think and tell you later."

Every Life Insurance agent hears this sentence regularly. It is polite, but it also creates uncertainty. Many agents feel discouraged and assume the customer is not interested. In reality, most of these customers are not refusing — they are postponing.

Postponement is the biggest competitor of insurance.

People delay insurance not because they disagree, but because there is no visible urgency today. Daily work, expenses, and comfort take priority, while protection planning is pushed to the future.

Your role is not to pressure the customer.

Your role is to gently highlight the importance of the present.

1. Understand the Meaning of 'Later'

"Later" usually means one of three things:

- The customer did not fully understand
- The customer is confused about the amount
- The customer has not felt urgency

Find the real reason politely.

You may ask:

"Certainly, sir. So that I can assist properly, may I know what you would like to consider more — the plan details or the saving amount?"

This helps the customer express the real concern.

2. Give Time, But Not Distance

If you immediately stop follow-up, the decision disappears. If you call daily, the customer feels pressure.

Instead, agree on a specific time:

"I will call you on Sunday evening after you discuss with your family."

A fixed follow-up shows professionalism and keeps the discussion alive.

3. Gentle Reminder Method

During follow-up, do not repeat the entire presentation. Give a short reminder connected to the responsibility.

Example:

"I just wanted to remind you about the education protection plan we discussed for your child's future. Planning early makes it easier and more comfortable."

Short and meaningful reminders are effective.

4. Use Future Visualisation

Help the customer imagine a future situation:

"Five years later, you will feel relaxed knowing this was already arranged."

This shifts thinking from present comfort to future security.

5. Offer Comfortable Options

Sometimes hesitation is due to affordability. Offer a smaller beginning:

"Let us start with a comfortable amount now. We can increase protection later as your income grows."

Starting removes the delay.

6. Avoid Negative Reaction

Never show disappointment or irritation. If the customer feels judged, he will avoid further communication. Stay positive and respectful.

Patience converts postponement into a decision.

7. Maintain Relationship

Even if the customer delays for months, maintain occasional contact — festival greetings, useful reminders, or a short courtesy call. Familiarity reduces hesitation.

People often decide with the person who stayed in contact.

Important Principle

Today's "later" is tomorrow's "why didn't I start earlier?"

Many people regret postponing protection after a life event. Your responsibility is to help them act before regret.

An insurance decision is rarely urgent in appearance, but always urgent in importance.

Do not chase the customer.

Do not forget the customer.

Guide the customer.

Follow up with care, not pressure.

Consistency builds memory.

Memory builds trust.

Trust builds decision.

The agent who patiently follows up is the agent who consistently succeeds.

Later becomes now, when understanding becomes clear.

CHAPTER 21

THE ART OF FOLLOW-UP

In the Life Insurance profession, the first meeting creates interest, but the follow-up creates a decision.

Most customers do not decide immediately. Not because they disagree, but because life is busy. Work pressure, family matters, and daily responsibilities make them postpone planning. If the agent does not follow up properly, the discussion slowly disappears from the customer's mind.

Follow-up is not a reminder for your business.

Follow-up is a reminder for their protection.

1. Why Follow-Up is Necessary

After your meeting, the customer returns to their routine life. Your discussion about future planning becomes less important compared to daily activities. A polite follow-up brings the importance back to attention.

People rarely refuse permanently.

They simply forget temporarily.

Your follow-up refreshes awareness.

2. The Biggest Mistake

Two extreme mistakes happen:

- No follow-up — the customer forgets
- Too frequent follow-up — the customer feels irritated

Both reduce success.

Correct follow-up means gentle, periodic, and meaningful contact.

3. Fix the Next Contact Before Leaving

Never end a meeting without deciding the next communication.

Example:

"I will call you on Wednesday evening after you discuss with your family."

A pre-decided follow-up feels professional, rather than intrusive.

4. First Follow-Up

Do not repeat the full presentation. Speak briefly:

"Sir, I just wanted to check if you had time to think about the family protection plan we discussed."

Short and respectful follow-up works best.

5. What to Speak During Follow-Up

Follow-up should not sound like a collection call. Connect it to benefit:

"I remembered our discussion about your child's education planning and thought to check if you needed any clarification."

Benefit-based follow-up creates interest.

6. Best Times to Follow-Up

- Evening hours
- Weekend mornings
- After salary dates

Avoid early mornings or late nights. Respecting time increases response.

7. Use Different Methods

Follow-up need not always be a call:

- Short message
- Festival greeting
- Birthday wishes
- Helpful reminder

Relationship-based contact keeps the connection alive.

8. The Follow-Up Cycle

First reminder — within 2 days.

Second reminder — after 5 to 7 days.

Third reminder — after 2 weeks.

Later — occasional relationship contact.

Consistency is more important than frequency.

9. Never Sound Desperate

Avoid speaking as if you urgently need the policy. Speak as if you are concerned about their planning.

Confidence attracts decisions.

10. After Decision

Once the customer agrees, act quickly. Complete documentation without delay. Quick service strengthens trust and reduces second thoughts.

Important Understanding

Many agents stop after one or two attempts. Successful agents continue politely until the customer decides. Often, the decision comes after the fourth or fifth contact.

Follow-up is not chasing.

Follow-up is caring.

People do not always buy from the first agent they meet.

They buy from the agent who stayed connected.

Every polite reminder keeps you remembered.

Every remembered agent receives business.

Therefore:

Meet once → Known.

Follow-up twice → Familiar.

Follow-up regularly → Trusted.

And trusted agents never struggle for policies.

CHAPTER 22

CLOSING THE POLICY CONFIDENTLY

A successful Life Insurance meeting has one clear purpose — helping the customer decide for family protection. Many agents hesitate at this moment. They explain everything properly, but at the end, they simply say, “Think and tell me.” The discussion ends without direction.

If you do not ask for the decision, the customer assumes the decision is not important now.

Closing is not pressure.

Closing is clarity.

You are not forcing a purchase. You are helping the customer start protection.

1. Recognise Buying Signals

Before closing, observe signs that the customer is ready:

- Asking about the premium amount
- Asking about payment mode
- Asking about start date
- Discussing with spouse
- Re-reading the illustration

These are signals of interest. This is the right time to guide the decision.

2. Do Not Delay the Moment

Many agents continue explaining even after the customer understands. Too much talking creates confusion again. When the customer is clear, move to closing politely.

Clarity should lead to action.

3. The Assumptive Close

Instead of asking, "Will you take the policy?" use guiding choices:

"Would monthly saving be comfortable or yearly saving?"

"Shall we start the protection from this month?"

The customer feels the decision is natural.

4. The Summary Close

Briefly repeat the benefit:

"We discussed your family's financial safety and children's future education support. This plan ensures both protection and a future fund. We can start the arrangement today."

Then pause. Silence allows a decision.

5. The Responsibility Close

Use gentle responsibility:

"Planning done today gives peace of mind from tomorrow."

This reminds of the importance without pressure.

6. Handle Last-Minute Hesitation

If the customer hesitates:

"I understand this is an important step. That is exactly why starting early helps your family more."

Stay calm and supportive.

7. Documentation Confidence

When the customer agrees, immediately guide documentation. Speak positively:

"I will help you complete the formalities. It will take only a few minutes."

Smooth process prevents second thoughts.

8. After Closing

Congratulate sincerely:

"You have taken a very responsible decision for your family."

This reinforces satisfaction and trust.

Important Understanding

Customers rarely regret taking protection.

They often regret delaying protection.

Your job is not to collect a signature.

Your job is to help a family feel secure.

A confident agent closes naturally because his intention is clear.

Do not feel shy to ask for a decision.

You are not taking money away.

You are creating safety.

The right explanation creates understanding.

Right timing creates a decision.

Right closing creates policy.

And every policy is a promise fulfilled.

CHAPTER 23

AFTER-SALES SERVICE AND RELATIONSHIP BUILDING

In the Life Insurance profession, business does not end after issuing a policy. In fact, real business begins after the policy.

Many agents focus only on completing the proposal and collecting the first premium. After that, they disappear until the next target month. This is the biggest mistake. A policy gives commission once, but a relationship gives business for years.

Service creates a relationship.

Relationships create referrals.

1. First Contact After Policy

Within a few days after policy issuance, contact the customer:

"Your policy document has arrived. I just wanted to ensure everything is clear and comfortable."

This simple call shows responsibility and care.

2. Explain Policy Clearly

Sit with the customer and explain:

- Premium dates
- Payment methods
- Nomination details
- Contact procedure

A customer who understands the policy feels confident. Confidence creates long-term trust.

3. Premium Reminder Service

Before every due date, remind politely:

"Your family protection premium is due next week. I just wanted to help you avoid any interruption."

This is not a collection call. It is a service reminder. Customers appreciate agents who help them maintain continuity.

4. Personal Connection

Maintain periodic friendly contact:

- Birthday wishes
- Festival greetings
- Anniversary greetings

These are not small gestures. They create an emotional connection.

People remember the person who remembers them.

5. Assist During Changes

Help customers during important updates:

- Address change
- Mobile number change
- Nominee update
- Loan assistance

When you help without expecting immediate business, trust becomes permanent.

6. Claim Support — The Most Important Moment

The real value of a life insurance agent appears during a claim. In difficult times, the family may not know procedures. Your guidance and presence give emotional and financial support.

At that moment, you are not an agent.

You are a supporter of the family.

Families never forget such help.

7. Policy Review Meetings

Once a year, meet the client and review planning:

"Your responsibilities have increased. Let us check if your protection is still sufficient."

This naturally creates additional business.

8. Ask for Referrals Politely

After good service, you may ask:

"If you know any friend or relative who may benefit from such planning, please feel free to connect me."

Satisfied customers happily refer.

9. Build Long-Term Relationship

Do not treat customers as transactions. Treat them as relationships. When they trust you, they will contact you first for any financial decision.

Relationships reduce marketing effort.

Important Understanding

A new customer requires effort.

An existing customer requires care.

Care is easier than marketing.

After-sales service turns a one-time client into a lifelong connection.

A policy gives income today.

A relationship gives income every year.

Serve sincerely.

Support patiently.

Stay connected.

When customers feel you stand with them even after business, you become not just a Life Insurance agent — you become their family advisor.

And a family advisor never searches for business.

Business automatically comes to him.

CHAPTER 24

DAILY ACTIVITY SYSTEM FOR LIFE INSURANCE AGENTS

Many Life Insurance agents work very hard for a few days and then become inactive for many days. Because of this irregular activity, income also becomes irregular. The truth is simple — insurance business rewards consistency more than talent.

Small daily actions create big yearly results.

Successful agents do not depend on mood, season, or target pressure. They follow a daily system. When activity becomes a habit, performance becomes predictable.

1. Understand the Business Cycle

Every policy comes through a process:

Contact → Meeting → Discussion → Decision → Policy.

If you want more policies, you must increase the first step — contacts.

No contacts mean no meetings.

No meetings mean no business.

2. The Daily 5–3–2 Rule

Follow a simple daily formula:

5 New Contacts.

3 Follow-Up Calls.

2 Face-to-Face Meetings.

If you follow this regularly, business will never stop.

3. Morning Routine

Start your day with preparation:

- Review your goals
- Plan whom to meet
- Arrange documents
- Practice your opening lines

Do not start the day without a plan. Planned days produce productive results.

4. Prospecting Time

Dedicate fixed hours to contacting new people. This is the most important activity. Many agents avoid prospecting because of hesitation, but this is the foundation of success.

New people bring new opportunities.

5. Follow-Up Time

Keep a specific time every day only for follow-up calls. Do not mix it with other work. Follow-up maintains continuity and converts interest into decisions.

Follow-up is not optional work.

It is essential work.

6. Meeting Preparation

Before every meeting:

- Know the customer's name and background
- Decide your discussion purpose
- Carry necessary materials neatly

Preparation increases confidence.

7. Record Keeping

Maintain a simple diary or notebook:

- Whom you contacted
- Whom you met
- Who needs follow-up

Memory can fail. Written record guides action.

8. Weekly Review

At the end of each week, review:

How many contacts?

How many meetings?

How many decisions?

If results are low, increase activity — not excuses.

9. Avoid Common Mistakes

- Waiting for the month-end to work
- Working only when the target pressure comes
- Depending only on known people

Consistent daily effort is stronger than last-minute effort.

10. The Activity Truth

Income in Life Insurance is not decided by one day's work.

It is decided by your daily habits.

You may not see immediate results for every contact, but each effort builds your future pipeline.

Seeds planted today become policies later.

Golden Formula

Regular Activity → Regular Meetings → Regular Decisions → Regular Income.

Motivation may change daily.

Habit remains daily.

Therefore, do not depend only on motivation. Create a routine. When routine becomes discipline, success becomes natural.

Meet people every day.

Guide sincerely every day.

Improve gradually every day.

Do this consistently, and the profession will reward you with stability, respect, and growth.

Success in Life Insurance is not mysterious.

It is systematic.

CHAPTER 25

TIME MANAGEMENT FOR FIELD SUCCESS

Every Life Insurance agent receives the same 24 hours in a day. Yet some agents consistently achieve targets while others struggle. The difference is not area, contacts, or luck. The difference is how time is used.

Time is the real capital of an agent.

In this profession, money does not create business first. Time invested in the right activity creates business.

1. The Common Problem

Many agents spend most of the day on low-result activities:

- Sitting in the office waiting for customers
- Long conversations with friends
- Unplanned travel
- Repeated discussion with one doubtful client

At the end of the day, they feel busy but not productive.

Busy does not always mean effective.

2. Understand Productive Hours

The most productive hours for meeting customers are:

Morning: 8:00 AM – 10:30 AM

Evening: 5:30 PM – 8:30 PM

During these times, people are more available and relaxed. Use these hours only for appointments and visits.

3. Divide the Day Properly

A simple daily structure:

Morning → New contacts and appointment fixing.

Afternoon → Follow-up calls and preparation.

Evening → Client meetings.

When time has a purpose, work becomes organised.

4. Appointment System

Do not visit randomly. Fix appointments in advance. Random visits waste travel time and energy. A confirmed meeting increases the success rate and saves effort.

Planned meetings produce planned results.

5. Limit Unproductive Activities

Avoid spending excessive time on:

- Social media browsing
- Waiting in tea shops
- Re-explaining repeatedly to uninterested prospects

Give attention where decision possibilities exist.

6. The 80/20 Principle

In practice, 20% of activities create 80% of results.

High-value activities:

- Meeting new people
- Follow-ups
- Presentations

Low-value activities:

- Paper arranging for long hours
- Complaining about the market
- Discussing problems without action

Focus on high-value activities daily.

7. Weekly Planning

Every Sunday evening, plan the coming week:

- Whom to meet
- Whom to call
- Where to visit

Planning reduces confusion and increases confidence.

8. Control Procrastination

Do not postpone important actions. The call you delay today may be the policy you miss tomorrow.

Immediate action creates opportunity.

9. Personal Discipline

Start work at a fixed time daily. Do not wait for mood or motivation. Discipline protects your schedule from distractions.

Time respected becomes time productive.

10. End-of-Day Review

Before finishing the day, ask:

Did I meet new people today?

Did I follow up?

Did I move any decision forward?

If yes, the day was successful.

Important Understanding

You cannot control customer decisions.

You can control your daily actions.

When actions are consistent, results follow naturally.

A life insurance agent who manages time well rarely experiences income uncertainty. He always has future business in the pipeline.

Use your time wisely.

Because every hour used properly today becomes income tomorrow.

Time wasted is opportunity lost. Time managed is success created.

CHAPTER 26

TELE-CALLING AND APPOINTMENT FIXING

For a life insurance agent, the telephone is not just a communication tool. It is a meeting-fixing tool. The purpose of a call is not to sell a policy. The purpose is to get an appointment.

Never try to explain insurance fully on the phone.

The phone is for a meeting. The meeting is for discussion. Discussion is for decision.

When agents try to sell on the phone, customers quickly end the call. When agents try to fix a meeting, customers listen longer.

1. Before Calling

Prepare yourself:

- Know the person's name
- Decide your opening line
- Keep a pen and diary ready
- Smile before speaking (your voice changes)

Confidence in voice creates interest.

2. Correct Opening

Start politely:

"Good evening, sir. Am I speaking with Mr Ramesh?"

(Wait for confirmation)

"Sir, my name is Sathya Prakash Urs S N. I work in family financial protection and future planning services."

Pause for a second. Let the person listen.

3. State the Purpose Clearly

"I am not calling to sell anything on the phone. I just wanted to meet you for 10 minutes to discuss children's education and family security planning."

This reduces resistance immediately.

4. Give Time Choice

Instead of asking "Are you free?", give options:

"Which is more comfortable for you — evening or weekend morning?"

Choice encourages response.

5. If Customer Says Busy

Reply politely:

"No problem, sir. Please suggest a convenient day. I will adjust accordingly."

Respect creates acceptance.

6. Reference Method

If you have a contact reference:

"Your friend Mr Kumar suggested I speak with you regarding family protection planning."

Reference increases trust.

7. Handling Rejection on Call

If the person says not interested:

"I understand, sir. I only wanted to introduce myself. In future, if you ever need guidance regarding protection planning, I will be happy to assist."

End respectfully. Some people later respond positively.

8. Keep the Call Short

2–3 minutes is ideal. Long calls reduce interest. The goal is appointment, not explanation.

Short call → Higher chance of meeting.

9. Confirmation Message

After fixing the appointment, send a polite message:

"Thank you for your time today. I will meet you tomorrow at 6:30 PM as discussed."

Professionalism increases credibility.

10. Important Telephone Rules

- Speak slowly and clearly
- Do not argue
- Do not insist repeatedly
- Always thank before ending

Your voice represents your personality.

Key Principle

A phone call should create comfort, not pressure.

When comfort is created, a meeting happens.

More calls → More meetings → More discussions → More policies.

Do not fear calling.

Each call is a new opportunity.

You are not disturbing people.

You are offering guidance.

A confident call opens a door.

An open door leads to a relationship.

And relationships create business.

CHAPTER 27

USING REFERRALS TO EXPAND BUSINESS

In the Life Insurance profession, the easiest prospect is not a stranger. The easiest prospect is a referred person.

Cold contacts require effort to build trust.

Referred contacts already have partial trust.

A referral means someone has spoken positively about you. Because of that, the new person listens to you with comfort.

1. Why Referrals are Important

Referred customers:

- Listen patiently
- Trust faster
- Decide earlier
- Give further references

One good client can open many doors.

2. When to Ask for a Referral

Do not ask immediately after the first meeting. Ask about satisfaction — usually after policy completion or after helping in service.

The best moment is when the customer feels happy with your support.

3. How to Ask Politely

Do not ask directly:

"Give me 5 contacts."

Instead say:

"If you know any friend or relative who may benefit from such family protection planning, please feel free to introduce me. I will guide them sincerely."

This sounds respectful and service-oriented.

4. Make It Easy for the Customer

People want to help but hesitate to share numbers. Offer simple options:

"I can call only after you inform them."

"Or you may share my number with them."

Comfort increases response.

5. Use Appreciation

After receiving a referral:

"Thank you for trusting me and connecting me. I will take good care while guiding them."

Always maintain the reputation given by the referrer.

6. Handle Referred Person Carefully

When meeting a referred contact:

Mention the referrer:

"Mr Ramesh suggested I meet you regarding family financial planning."

The new person feels safe because someone they know recommended you.

7. Never Break Trust

Do not pressure referred contacts. If they feel uncomfortable, it affects your existing client relationship. Handle with patience and respect.

Trust spreads faster than advertising.

8. Build Referral Habit

After every satisfied service:

- Policy completion
- Claim help
- Premium assistance

Politely ask for a reference. Make it a regular practice.

9. Referral Record

Maintain a list:

Who referred whom?

Thank the original customer later. Appreciation strengthens connection.

10. The Referral Cycle

Good service → Customer satisfaction → Referral → New client → Good service again.

This cycle creates continuous business without heavy marketing.

Important Understanding

A stranger doubts you first.

A referred person trusts you first.

Referral business grows faster and lasts longer.

Advertising creates awareness.

Service creates a recommendation.

Therefore, focus on serving existing clients sincerely. When they trust you deeply, they naturally introduce you to others.

Your reputation becomes your marketing.

An agent with a strong reputation never struggles for prospects.

CHAPTER 28

COMMUNICATION SKILLS FOR ADVISORS

In the Life Insurance profession, success depends less on what you know and more on how you communicate. Many agents have good knowledge but struggle because their message does not reach the customer clearly.

Communication is not only about speaking.

Communication is making the other person understand.

A customer decides not when you finish talking, but when he clearly understands your meaning.

1. Speak Simple, Not Complex

Avoid difficult financial words and technical explanations. Speak in everyday language. Customers appreciate clarity more than intelligence.

Simple speaking creates a strong understanding.

Instead of impressing the customer with information, connect with meaning.

2. Listen Actively

Listening is the most powerful part of communication. When the customer speaks, give full attention. Do not interrupt. Do not prepare your next sentence while he is talking.

Nod gently and acknowledge:

"I understand."

"That is a valid concern."

Listening makes the customer comfortable and cooperative.

3. Use the Customer's Name

Use the customer's name naturally during conversation:

"Mr Ramesh, your concern about children's education is very important."

This creates a personal connection.

4. Maintain Positive Tone

Your tone should be calm and respectful. Avoid sounding too serious or too casual. A friendly and professional tone builds trust.

People trust how you say more than what you say.

5. Avoid Argument

If the customer disagrees, do not argue. Respectfully respond:

"That is a good point. Let us also consider this aspect."

Agreement first, explanation next.

6. Control Speaking Speed

Speaking too fast shows nervousness. Speaking too slowly shows uncertainty. Maintain moderate speed with small pauses.

Pauses give thinking time.

7. Ask and Confirm

After explaining, confirm understanding:

"Is this clear?"

"Would you like me to explain differently?"

This ensures communication is complete.

8. Non-Verbal Communication

Communication includes body language:

- Smile
- Eye contact

- Open posture
- Gentle hand movement

Your behaviour should show confidence and sincerity.

9. Avoid Negative Words

Avoid phrases like:
"Problem," "Loss," "Danger"

Use softer words:
"Risk," "Safety," "Security"

Positive words create acceptance.

10. End Positively

Always end the discussion with a reassuring statement:
"This planning will give peace of mind to your family."

A positive ending leaves a positive memory.

Important Understanding

Customers may forget your explanation.

They remember your behaviour.

A polite, patient, and respectful agent is always welcome again.

Communication is not a performance.

It is a connection.

When the connection becomes strong, trust grows.

When trust grows, decisions follow naturally.

Therefore, improve not only your knowledge, but also your way of expressing it.

Clear communication → Better understanding → Stronger trust → More policies.

A good communicator becomes a successful advisor.

CHAPTER 29

BODY LANGUAGE AND VOICE MODULATION

Communication is not only words. A large part of communication happens without speaking. Customers observe your face, posture, hand movement, and tone of voice even before they listen to your explanation.

Your body speaks before your words.

If your words are confident but your body language shows nervousness, the customer believes your body, not your words. Therefore, controlling body language and voice is an important professional skill for a Life Insurance agent.

1. Posture

Sit straight but relaxed. Do not lean too far forward or backwards. A balanced posture shows confidence and stability. Slouching shows disinterest, and stiffness shows tension.

Comfortable posture creates comfortable conversation.

2. Eye Contact

Maintain natural eye contact while speaking and listening. Do not stare continuously, and do not keep looking down at papers. Balanced eye contact shows honesty and confidence.

People trust the person who looks at them while speaking.

3. Facial Expression

Keep a gentle smile. A serious or worried face makes the customer uncomfortable. A pleasant expression makes the environment friendly and open.

A smile reduces hesitation.

4. Hand Movements

Use simple and limited hand gestures while explaining. Avoid pointing fingers or moving hands excessively. Controlled gestures help emphasise points without distraction.

Calm movements show self-control.

5. Avoid Nervous Habits

Do not repeatedly check your phone, tap the table, shake your leg, or play with a pen. These habits show nervousness and reduce credibility.

Stillness creates confidence.

6. Voice Modulation

Your voice should be clear, warm, and steady. Avoid speaking in a monotone voice. Slight variation in tone keeps attention and interest.

Speak slightly slower than normal conversation speed. Clear speech improves understanding.

7. Volume Control

Do not speak too loudly or too softly. A moderate volume sounds professional. If your voice is too soft, the customer may not follow. If too loud, the customer may feel pressured.

Balanced volume creates comfort.

8. Pause Effectively

After explaining an important point, pause for a moment. Silence allows the customer to think and absorb the message.

Silence is also part of communication.

9. Listening Signals

While listening, nod gently and maintain attention. This shows respect and involvement. Customers feel valued when they see you are listening sincerely.

Listening to body language builds connection.

10. Ending Impression

Stand up calmly, thank the customer, and leave with a smile. Your final behaviour is the last memory of the meeting.

The last impression influences future decisions.

Important Understanding

Customers may not remember your exact words.

They remember how you made them feel.

Your body language creates comfort.

Your voice creates clarity.

Comfort and clarity create trust.

Therefore, practice speaking in front of a mirror. Observe your posture, expression, and tone. With practice, confidence becomes natural.

When your body language is calm, and your voice is clear, your message becomes powerful.

A confident appearance leads to a confident response.

And confident response leads to a positive decision.

CHAPTER 30

ETHICS AND HONESTY IN INSURANCE BUSINESS

In the insurance profession, knowledge brings business for a short time, but character brings business for a lifetime.

Customers may initially come because of a plan, but they stay because of trust. Trust does not come from clever speaking. Trust comes from honesty.

Insurance is a promise for the future. Therefore, the person who explains it must be truthful in the present.

1. Tell the Truth Always

Explain the plan clearly — benefits as well as conditions. Do not hide waiting periods, payment requirements, or limitations. A customer who understands correctly remains satisfied.

A misinformed customer becomes disappointed.

Honesty may take a little more effort today, but it prevents serious problems tomorrow.

2. Never Overpromise

Avoid statements like:

"Guaranteed high returns"

"Double money quickly"

Such promises create wrong expectations. When expectations are not met, the relationship breaks.

Correct expectation creates long-term respect.

3. Recommend Suitable Plans

Do not suggest a large premium only for higher commission. Suggest a plan that the customer can comfortably continue. A lapsed policy harms both the customer and your reputation.

The right plan is better than a big plan.

4. Proper Documentation

Fill proposal forms carefully. Ensure health details and personal information are accurate. Incorrect details may create claim difficulties in the future.

Careful work protects families.

5. Protect Customer Confidentiality

Customers share personal and financial details with you. Never discuss their information with others. Confidentiality shows professionalism.

Respecting privacy increases confidence.

6. Service Responsibility

Help during policy servicing and especially during claims. This is the moment when your honesty is truly tested. Support the family patiently and sincerely.

Service proves sincerity.

7. Do Not Criticise Competitors

Never speak negatively about other agents or companies. Speak positively about your service and guidance. Respectful behaviour increases dignity.

Professionalism earns respect.

8. Long-Term Thinking

Quick commission gives temporary satisfaction. A good reputation gives continuous income. When people trust you, they recommend you to others.

Reputation becomes your advertisement.

9. Admit Mistakes

If you make an error, accept it and correct it immediately. Customers appreciate responsibility more than perfection.

Accountability builds credibility.

10. The Real Reward

In this profession, the greatest reward is not only income. It is a blessing. When a family receives support because of your guidance, you become part of their gratitude.

Important principle:

Policy gives a commission once.

Integrity gives commission forever.

Final Thought

Work in such a way that when people hear your name, they feel confident. Let your identity be honesty, service, and reliability.

An honest agent may grow slowly in the beginning, but grows steadily and permanently.

Truth builds trust.

Trust builds a relationship.

Relationships build success.

And success built on honesty never collapses.

CHAPTER 31

HANDLING REJECTION POSITIVELY

Rejection is a natural part of the Life Insurance profession. Every agent, whether new or experienced, hears "no" many times. Some agents become discouraged and slow down. Others continue with confidence and succeed. The difference is not opportunity — it is attitude.

Rejection is not failure.

Rejection is feedback.

A customer who refuses is not rejecting you as a person. He is only postponing or declining the proposal at that moment. Taking it personally reduces confidence unnecessarily.

1. Change Your Thinking

Do not think: "I failed."

Think: "I learned."

Each discussion teaches something — a better explanation, a clearer question, or a different approach. Every meeting improves your skills.

Experience grows through attempts.

2. Do Not Argue

If a customer refuses, accept politely:

"I understand. Thank you for your time."

Arguing damages your image and closes future opportunities. A respectful exit keeps the door open.

A polite departure creates a second chance.

3. Maintain Relationship

After rejection, do not avoid the customer. Continue normal greeting during meetings or occasions. Familiarity reduces hesitation later.

Many future clients are today's refusers.

4. Separate Emotion from Work

Do not carry one rejection to the next meeting. Every customer is a new beginning. Confidence should remain steady.

One "no" should not stop the next "yes."

5. Increase Activity

Confidence does not grow by thinking. It grows by action. Meeting more people reduces the emotional effect of any single rejection.

More attempts reduce fear.

6. Learn From Each Case

After a refusal, review:

Did the customer understand?

Was the need clear?

Did I close at the right time?

Learning converts rejection into improvement.

7. Stay Positive

Avoid negative self-talk such as:

"This profession is difficult"

"People are not interested"

Replace with:

"I am improving daily"

"I will meet the right customer"

Thoughts influence performance.

8. Build Emotional Strength

Remember why you joined this profession — to help families and build a career. Keep your purpose stronger than temporary disappointment.

Purpose gives persistence.

9. The Numbers Truth

In practice, not every person will accept. Out of several discussions, a few become policies. This is normal in every advisory profession.

Rejection is part of the process, not the end of the process.

10. Keep Moving

After a refusal, immediately move to the next activity. Action removes negative feelings quickly.

Waiting increases doubt.

Action increases confidence.

Important Understanding

The agent who avoids rejection avoids success.

The agent who accepts rejection approaches success.

Every "no" brings experience.

Every experience improves communication.

Improved communication brings "yes."

Therefore, welcome rejection as a teacher.

Do not count how many refused.

Count how many you met.

Because every meeting is a step forward.

Stay patient.

Stay active.

Stay positive.

Success does not come to the agent who never hears "no."

Success comes to the agent who continues after hearing "no."

And persistence always wins.

CHAPTER 32

MOTIVATION AND SELF-DISCIPLINE

Many Life Insurance agents work with great energy for a few days, especially near the end of the month. After achieving or missing the target, their activity reduces. This cycle repeats again and again. The real problem is not lack of ability — it is lack of sustained motivation and discipline.

Motivation starts action.

Discipline continues action.

If you depend only on motivation, your performance changes with mood. If you develop discipline, your performance becomes steady.

1. Understand the Truth About Motivation

Motivation is temporary. Some days you feel energetic, some days you do not. Waiting for the "right mood" is dangerous in this profession. Customers do not know your mood; they respond only to your activity.

Work even when you do not feel like working.

Action creates motivation, not the opposite.

2. Create a Daily Habit

Fix a minimum daily activity. For example:

- Speak to at least five new people daily
- Do follow-up calls daily
- Meet at least one person daily

Even on a low-energy day, complete this minimum. Habit builds momentum.

A small daily effort prevents long gaps.

3. Set Personal Goals

Do not work only for company targets. Set your own goals:

- Income goal
- Family support goal
- Lifestyle goal

When goals are personal, effort becomes meaningful.

4. Morning Self-Preparation

Start the day positively:

- Read a motivational thought
- Review your plan
- Visualise a successful meeting

A positive morning influences the whole day.

5. Avoid a Negative Environment

Avoid people who constantly complain:

"Market is bad"

"No one buys insurance"

Negative conversations reduce enthusiasm. Spend time with positive, active individuals.

The environment affects performance.

6. Reward Yourself

After achieving a weekly goal, give yourself a small reward — a good meal, a short outing, or rest. Recognition encourages continuation.

Progress should be celebrated.

7. Control Procrastination

The biggest enemy of success is postponing important actions. The call you delay today becomes the missed opportunity tomorrow.

Do important work first.

8. Maintain Health

Good health supports good performance. Proper sleep, simple exercise, and balanced food improve energy and confidence.

Energy improves communication.

9. Keep Learning

Attend training programs, read books, and observe successful agents. Learning refreshes enthusiasm and improves skill.

Growth keeps interest alive.

10. Remember Your Purpose

This profession is not only about income. It is about helping families stay financially safe. When you remember the value of your work, your motivation strengthens.

Purpose is stronger than pressure.

Important Principle

Successful agents do not wait for motivation.

They create a routine.

Routine creates discipline.

Discipline creates consistency.

Consistency creates success.

Some days will be difficult. Some meetings will fail. But if you continue your daily activities steadily, results will surely appear.

Do not depend on occasional effort.

Depend on daily effort.

A little work every day is better than a lot of work one day.

Stay steady.

Stay focused.

Stay disciplined.

Because in the Life Insurance profession, winners are not the most talented — they are the most consistent.

CHAPTER 33

HOW SUCCESSFUL AGENTS THINK AND WORK

In every Life Insurance office, you will find two types of agents. Some struggle month after month, while some consistently achieve results and earn respect. They work in the same market, meet similar people, and use the same products. Yet their outcomes are very different.

The difference is not opportunity.

The difference is in thinking and working style.

Successful agents do not do different things.

They do common things differently and consistently.

1. Thinking About the Profession

Average agent: "I am selling policies."

Successful agent: "I am protecting families."

This one belief changes confidence, communication, and commitment.

2. Attitude Toward Work

The average agent works when the target pressure comes.

A successful agent works daily, regardless of the target.

Regular activity builds steady business.

3. Approach to Customers

The average agent explains plans immediately.

A successful agent first understands the customer's life and responsibilities.

Understanding creates connection.

4. Reaction to Rejection

The average agent feels discouraged after a refusal.

A successful agent treats refusal as part of the process and continues.

Persistence builds experience.

5. Prospecting Habit

An average agent depends on known contacts.

A successful agent meets new people continuously.

New contacts create new opportunities.

6. Follow-Up Behaviour

The average agent follows up once or twice and stops.

A successful agent follows up politely and consistently.

Consistency converts interest into a decision.

7. Learning Attitude

The average agent believes he already knows enough.

A successful agent keeps learning, improving communication, and observing seniors.

Learning improves performance.

8. Time Usage

The average agent spends time discussing problems.

A successful agent spends time meeting people.

Activity produces results.

9. Service After Policy

An average agent contacts only for new business.

A successful agent maintains relationships and supports service needs.

Service builds referrals.

10. Long-Term Vision

The average agent thinks about this month's commission.

A successful agent thinks about long-term reputation and client trust.

Reputation creates continuous income.

Daily Habits of Successful Agents

- Plan the day in advance
- Meet people every day
- Record activities
- Follow up regularly
- Maintain a positive attitude

They treat this profession as a career, not temporary work.

Important Understanding

Top agents are not born confident.

They become confident through daily action.

They may start with hesitation, but they do not stop. With each meeting, they improve. With each improvement, results grow.

Success is not a sudden event.

It is a repeated behaviour.

If you adopt their habits, you can achieve similar results.

The market is not different for successful agents.

Their mindset is different.

Work sincerely.

Meet consistently.

Serve patiently.

Over time, your name will be associated with reliability. When people think about financial protection, they will remember you.

Do not compare your beginning with someone's achievement.

Compare your daily effort with yesterday's effort.

Improve a little every day, and success will follow.

Successful agents are ordinary people with extraordinary consistency.

And consistency always creates success.

CHAPTER 34

THE IMPORTANCE OF CHILD HIGHER EDUCATION PLANNING

Securing the Future of the Next Generation

One of the greatest responsibilities of every parent is to ensure that their children receive **quality education**. Education shapes a child's future, builds confidence, creates opportunities, and enables them to lead a meaningful life. In today's world, **higher education has become one of the most important investments parents must plan for.**

However, many parents underestimate the **actual cost of higher education**. Due to inflation and increasing demand for professional courses, the cost of education is rising rapidly every year. Courses such as **engineering, medicine, management, data science, and international studies** can cost several lakhs or even crores in the future.

Therefore, responsible financial planning requires that parents start preparing early for their children's higher education.

This chapter explains **why child education planning is essential and how to calculate the required savings scientifically.**

Why Higher Education Planning is Necessary

Every parent dream of giving the best opportunities to their children. But dreams must be supported by **financial preparation**.

There are several reasons why education planning has become extremely important.

First, the **cost of higher education is increasing every year**. What costs ₹10 lakh today may cost ₹25 lakh or more after 15 years.

Second, many parents depend only on their **future income** without proper savings. If an unexpected financial crisis occurs, the child's education may suffer.

Third, proper planning ensures that the child can **choose the best course and institution without financial stress**.

Education planning therefore, becomes a **responsibility, not merely a financial goal**.

Understanding Education Inflation

Education inflation is generally higher than normal inflation. In many countries, education costs increase by approximately **8% to 10% every year**.

This means that the cost of a course doubles roughly every **8 to 9 years**.

For example, if a professional course costs **₹10 lakh today**, after 15 years, the cost may rise significantly due to inflation.

To calculate the future cost, we use the **Future Value formula**.

Future Cost = Present Cost × (1 + Inflation Rate) ^ Number of Years.

Example 1: Calculating Future Cost of Education

Let us assume the following situation.

The current cost of an engineering course is **₹10,00,000**.

The child is currently **3 years old**, and the course will be required at age **18**.

This means the investment horizon is **15 years**.

Assuming an education inflation rate of **8% per year**, we calculate the future cost.

Future Cost = 10,00,000 × (1.08) ^15

Future Cost ≈ **₹31,70,000**

This means that a course costing ₹10 lakh today may cost approximately **₹31–32 lakh after 15 years**.

Without proper planning, arranging this amount suddenly can become extremely difficult.

Example 2: Planning for a Medical Degree

Let us consider another example.

Suppose the current cost of a medical degree is **₹25,00,000**.

The child is **5 years old**, and the course will begin at age **18**, giving a time horizon of **13 years**.

Assuming an education inflation rate of **8%**, the future cost can be estimated.

Future Cost = 25,00,000 × (1.08) ^13

Future Cost ≈ **₹68,00,000**

This means that parents may need nearly **₹65–70 lakh** to support the child's medical education.

This example clearly shows how important **early financial planning** is.

How Much Should Parents Save Every Month?

Once the future cost is known, the next step is to determine **how much parents should save regularly**.

Suppose parents need **₹32 lakh after 15 years** for their child's education.

If they invest in a financial instrument that earns **10% annual return**, they can accumulate the required amount through systematic monthly investments.

For example, by investing approximately **₹8,000 per month for 15 years**, the parents may accumulate around **₹32 lakh**.

This demonstrates the power of **starting early and investing consistently**.

Small monthly investments made today can create a large education fund in the future.

The Risk of Not Planning

Many families postpone education planning because the goal seems far away. However, delaying planning can create serious problems later.

If parents start saving only when the child is **15 or 16 years old**, they will have very little time to accumulate the required funds. This may force them to take **loans or borrow money**, which can create financial stress.

Early planning avoids such difficulties and allows the family to achieve their goals comfortably.

The Role of Insurance in Education Planning

Life insurance plays a critical role in protecting the child's education plan.

If the earning parent is no longer alive due to an unforeseen event, the child's education should not stop. A well-designed insurance policy ensures that the education fund remains secure even in difficult circumstances.

This is why many financial planners recommend combining **education savings with life insurance protection**.

In this way, parents can ensure that their child's dreams remain protected under all circumstances.

A Message for Parents

Every child is born with potential. Education provides the knowledge and skills needed to transform that potential into achievement.

Parents who plan early for education give their children not only financial support but also **confidence and freedom to pursue their dreams**.

Education is not merely an expense; it is **an investment in the future of the next generation**.

Final Thought

A parent may not always be able to stay with their child throughout life, but proper planning ensures that their **dreams and support continue even in their absence**.

When parents believe in planning for their child's future, they take the first step toward securing it.

CHAPTER 35

RETIREMENT PLANNING CONCEPTS

Every earning person is working today, but one day earning will stop. This stage is called retirement. The biggest financial mistake people make is planning only for working years and ignoring non-working years.

Income stops at retirement.

Expenses do not stop at retirement.

Food, electricity, medical care, and daily living continue. In fact, medical expenses usually increase. Without proper planning, a person becomes dependent on children or relatives.

Retirement planning is not a luxury.

It is independence.

1. The Retirement Gap

During working years, income comes regularly. After retirement, the salary disappears. This creates a gap between income and expenses. Savings alone may not be sufficient for many years.

Customers must understand:

Retirement is certain, but retirement income is not automatic.

2. Why Early Planning Is Important

Starting early has three advantages:

- Small savings amount
- Long accumulation period
- Greater financial comfort

Starting late requires larger contributions and creates pressure.

Time is more powerful than amount.

3. Monthly Income Concept

Explain retirement not as a large lump sum but as a monthly income need.

Ask:

"After retirement, how much monthly amount will you need to maintain your lifestyle?"

When customers calculate, they realise planning is necessary.

4. Increasing Life Expectancy

People live longer today. Retirement may last 20–30 years. Without preparation, a long life can become a financial burden instead of a blessing.

Planning turns a long life into a peaceful life.

5. Protection + Pension

First protect the earning years, then secure the non-earning years. A complete financial plan includes both life protection and retirement income.

Working years need insurance.

Non-working years need a pension.

6. Emotional Benefit

Retirement planning is not only about money. It gives dignity. A financially independent person lives confidently without depending on others.

Independence gives self-respect.

7. Explaining Simply

Use a simple line:

"While working, your company gives a salary. After retirement, your planning should give a salary."

Customers easily understand this comparison.

8. Start With a Comfortable Amount

Encourage customers:

"Start small but start early."

Even a modest saving started early becomes meaningful later.

Important Understanding

People prepare carefully for their children's future, but often forget their own future. When retirement arrives without preparation, they face financial stress.

Your role is to remind gently, not alarmingly.

Retirement is not a distant event.

It is a predictable stage.

Planning and Preparing Today for a Secure Tomorrow

Retirement is one of the most important phases of human life. It is the stage when a person stops active employment and begins to live on the savings accumulated during the working years. After decades of hard work and responsibility, retirement should be a time of **peace, dignity, and financial independence**.

However, many people ignore retirement planning when they are young. They assume that their future income, children, or other sources will support them later in life. Unfortunately, this assumption often leads to financial difficulties during old age.

Therefore, **retirement planning is not a luxury—it is a necessity**.

Planning for retirement means preparing financially so that a person can maintain their lifestyle even after their regular income stops.

Why Retirement Planning is Essential

There are several reasons why retirement planning has become increasingly important in modern society.

First, **life expectancy has increased significantly** due to better healthcare and living conditions. Many people now live well into their seventies or eighties. This means retirement may last **20 to 30 years**, which requires substantial financial resources.

Second, the **cost of living continues to increase due to inflation**. The money that seems sufficient today may not be enough in the future.

Third, traditional family support systems are changing. In earlier generations, children often supported their parents financially. Today, many families live in different cities or countries, making it difficult to depend entirely on children for financial support.

For these reasons, every individual must take responsibility for their **own financial independence during retirement**.

Understanding the Retirement Gap

The retirement gap is the difference between **the income required during retirement and the savings available to support that income**.

If a person does not plan adequately, this gap can create financial stress in later years of life.

Retirement planning aims to eliminate this gap by building a sufficient **retirement corpus**, which is the total amount of money needed to support a person after retirement.

Estimating Monthly Retirement Needs

The first step in retirement planning is estimating how much money will be needed each month after retirement.

Financial planners often suggest that a person will require approximately **60% to 70% of their current income** during retirement to maintain a similar lifestyle.

This percentage accounts for daily expenses such as food, utilities, healthcare, transportation, and leisure activities.

Example 1: Estimating Retirement Needs

A person currently earns **₹80,000 per month**.

After retirement, he may require approximately **70% of his current income** to maintain his lifestyle.

Required retirement income:

₹80,000 × 70% = **₹56,000 per month**

This means he will need around **₹56,000 per month after retirement**.

Adjusting for Inflation

Inflation significantly affects retirement planning because the cost of living will increase over time.

Let us assume the person plans to retire after **25 years**, and inflation is **6% per year**.

Using the future value concept, the monthly expense of ₹56,000 today may grow substantially by the time retirement begins.

Future Monthly Expense ≈ **₹2,40,000 per month after 25 years**

This means that maintaining the same lifestyle in the future will require a much higher income due to inflation.

Calculating the Retirement Corpus

Once we estimate the future monthly expenses, we must calculate the **total amount of money required at retirement**.

Suppose a person retires at age **60** and expects to live until **80**, giving a retirement period of **20 years**.

If the required monthly income at retirement is ₹2,40,000, the annual requirement will be:
₹2,40,000 × 12 = **₹28,80,000 per year**

To sustain this income for 20 years, the retirement corpus required may be approximately **₹4 to ₹5 crore**, depending on investment returns and inflation adjustments.

This example shows that retirement planning requires **long-term discipline and systematic savings**.

Example 2: Starting Early Makes a Big Difference

Consider two individuals planning for retirement.

Person A begins saving **₹10,000 per month at age 30** and continues until age 60.

Person B begins saving **₹20,000 per month at age 45** and continues until age 60.

Even though Person B invests more money each month, Person A often accumulates a larger retirement corpus because of the **power of compounding over a longer time period**.

This example clearly shows that **starting early is the most powerful strategy in retirement planning**.

The Power of Compounding

Compounding is often called the **eighth wonder of the world** because it allows investments to grow exponentially over time.

When investments earn returns, and those returns are reinvested, the growth becomes faster year after year.

For example, if a person invests regularly and earns **10% annual return**, the money invested in the early years grows significantly over time.

This is why retirement planning should begin **as early as possible**, ideally during the first few years of employment.

The Role of Insurance in Retirement Planning

Life insurance and pension plans play an important role in retirement planning.

While savings and investments build the retirement corpus, insurance provides **financial protection against unexpected risks**.

Certain retirement-oriented insurance plans provide **regular pension income after retirement**, helping individuals maintain financial stability during their later years.

Combining savings, investments, and insurance creates a **balanced and secure retirement strategy**.

Retirement Planning Is Self-Respect

Retirement planning is not only about money. It is also about **self-respect and independence**.

A person who plans properly for retirement can live with dignity, make independent decisions, and avoid becoming a financial burden on others.

Financial independence in old age brings **peace of mind, confidence, and freedom**.

A Message for the Younger Generation

Many young people postpone retirement planning because retirement appears to be a distant goal. However, time passes quickly, and the best time to start planning is **today**.

Even small savings started early can grow into a large retirement fund over time.

The secret of successful retirement planning is **discipline, consistency, and patience**.

Final Reflection

Life is a journey with different stages. Childhood is a time for learning, youth is a time for building a career, and retirement should be a time for enjoying the fruits of one's hard work.

Those who plan wisely during their working years can look forward to a retirement filled with **security, comfort, and happiness**.

As with every meaningful achievement in life, the journey begins with belief.

Key Message

Earn today.

Save regularly.

Receive tomorrow.

A well-planned retirement ensures:

No financial worry

No dependency

No compromise in lifestyle

When customers understand retirement planning, they naturally value long-term policies.

Because everyone stops working one day.

But no one stops living one day.

And financial security makes living comfortably.

CHAPTER 36

PROTECTION PLANNING FOR FAMILIES

The primary purpose of life insurance is protection. Investment, savings, and tax benefits are additional advantages, but protection is the foundation.

Every family depends on income.

If income stops, difficulties start.

Protection planning means preparing in advance so that a family's life continues smoothly even during unexpected situations.

1. What is Protection Planning?

Protection planning is arranging financial support for the family if the earning member's income stops due to death, illness, or disability. It ensures that daily living, education, and responsibilities continue without major disturbance.

Planning removes uncertainty.

2. Monthly Needs of a Family

Every family has regular expenses:

- Food and groceries
- Rent or loan payment
- School or college fees
- Medical expenses
- Utility bills

These expenses continue regardless of circumstances. A family should not suddenly struggle because of one unexpected event.

Financial support gives emotional stability.

3. Income Replacement Concept

The earning member's income supports the entire household. Protection planning replaces that income for the family's needs.

Explain simply:

"Life insurance replaces your earning capacity when you are not able to earn."

This makes the purpose clear.

4. Loan and Liability Protection

If loans exist, the burden should not transfer to family members. Protection planning ensures liabilities are managed without stress.

Family should inherit security, not debt.

5. Peace of Mind

Financial uncertainty creates emotional stress. When a person knows his family is protected, he works peacefully and confidently.

Protection provides mental comfort.

6. Adequate Coverage

Having a small policy is good, but having adequate coverage is necessary. The protection amount should be sufficient to support the family for several years.

Incomplete planning gives incomplete safety.

7. Balanced Planning

Good planning includes:

- Protection during earning years
- Savings for future goals
- Income for retirement

Each stage of life requires preparation.

8. Role of the Agent

A life insurance agent helps families understand risks and arrange solutions. You are not forcing a product; you are offering security.

Your guidance prevents future hardship.

Important Understanding

People insure their house, vehicle, and valuables. But the most valuable asset is the earning ability of the family's provider.

Income is the engine of the household.

If the engine stops, the system stops. Protection planning ensures the system continues.

Human Life Value (HLV) – Understanding the True Worth of a Human Life

In the world of life insurance, one of the most important and meaningful concepts is **Human Life Value (HLV)**. Every insurance professional must understand this concept clearly, because it answers a very fundamental question:

"What is the financial value of a human life?"

When we ask this question, we are not trying to measure the emotional or moral value of a person. Human life is priceless and cannot be measured in emotional terms. However, from a financial perspective, every earning individual creates economic value for their family through the income they earn and the support they provide.

That economic contribution is what we call **Human Life Value**.

Human Life Value is the **present value of the future income that a person will generate for their family during the remaining working years of their life**. If the earning member suddenly passes away, the family not only loses a loved one, but they also lose the income that sustained their daily living, future goals, and financial security.

Life insurance exists to replace this lost income so that the family can continue their life with dignity and stability.

Why Human Life Value is Important?

Many people buy insurance without proper planning. Some purchase small policies based on what friends suggest. Others buy insurance simply because an agent recommended a particular product. Unfortunately, these decisions are often made without calculating the real financial requirements of the family.

Human Life Value brings **logic, clarity, and scientific thinking** into the process of insurance planning.

Instead of asking a client, *"How much premium can you pay?"*, a professional advisor asks a much more meaningful question:

"How much financial protection does your family actually need?"

HLV helps answer this question.

It ensures that the amount of insurance is not random but based on the **real economic value of the earning member's contribution to the family**.

The Basic Principle Behind HLV

Every earning person spends part of their income on themselves and contributes the remaining portion to their family. If the person dies, the personal expenses disappear, but the family still needs the financial support that the person used to provide.

Therefore, while calculating Human Life Value, we consider only the portion of income that benefits the family.

The basic formula is:

HLV = (Annual Income – Personal Expenses) × Remaining Working Years

This formula gives a simple estimate of the financial value that the earning person provides to the family over the course of their working life.

Example 1: Understanding HLV Through a Practical Case

Let us consider a person who is **35 years old** and plans to retire at the age of **60**.

His annual income is **₹10,00,000**. Out of this income, he spends **₹3,00,000** on personal expenses such as travel, hobbies, and personal lifestyle.

This means that the remaining **₹7,00,000** is used for the family's needs such as household expenses, children's education, and other financial responsibilities.

The person has **25 years of working life remaining**.

Using the HLV formula:

HLV = ₹7,00,000 × 25

HLV = **₹1,75,00,000**

This means that the financial value of his contribution to the family is approximately **₹1.75 crore**. Ideally, his life insurance protection should be around this amount so that if something happens to him, the family will still have the financial resources required to maintain their lifestyle.

Example 2: Another Illustration

Consider another example.

A person aged **40 years** earns **₹12,00,000 per year**. Out of this income, he spends **₹4,00,000** on his personal needs.

The amount he contributes to the family every year is:

₹12,00,000 – ₹4,00,000 = **₹8,00,000**

He plans to work until age **60**, which means he has **20 working years remaining**.

Using the HLV formula:

HLV = ₹8,00,000 × 20

HLV = **₹1,60,00,000**

In this case, the ideal life insurance protection should be approximately **₹1.6 crore**.

Factors That Influence Human Life Value

Human Life Value is not the same for everyone. It depends on several important factors.

The first factor is **age**. Younger individuals have more working years ahead of them, so their future income potential is greater.

The second factor is **income level**. Higher income naturally leads to a higher Human Life Value.

The third factor is the **number of dependents**. A person supporting a spouse, children, and elderly parents will have greater financial responsibilities.

The fourth factor is **future financial goals**, such as children's education, marriage expenses, and retirement planning.

All these factors must be considered when determining the correct level of life insurance protection.

The Advisor's Role in Explaining HLV

A professional insurance advisor does much more than sell policies. The advisor becomes a **financial guide for families**.

When advisors explain the concept of Human Life Value to clients, they help people understand the importance of protecting their income and securing their family's future.

Once clients clearly understand HLV, they no longer see insurance as an expense. Instead, they see it as **a responsibility and a necessity**.

This approach builds trust, strengthens relationships, and creates long-term credibility for the advisor.

A Simple Shortcut Used by Financial Planners

Although the Human Life Value method provides a detailed calculation, financial planners sometimes use a quick rule for estimation.

The recommended life insurance cover is usually **10 to 15 times the annual income**.

For example, if a person earns **₹10 lakh per year**, the suggested protection would be approximately **₹1 crore to ₹1.5 crore**.

This rule is helpful for quick discussions, but a detailed HLV calculation provides a much clearer and more accurate picture.

The Deeper Meaning of Human Life Value

Human Life Value teaches us a profound lesson about financial responsibility. Every earning individual carries the hopes and dreams of their family. Their income supports the daily life, education, health, and future security of their loved ones.

Protecting that income is one of the most important financial decisions a person can make.

Life insurance is not about predicting death. It is about **protecting life's responsibilities**.

Closing Reflection

Human life is priceless in emotional terms. No amount of money can replace the love, guidance, and presence of a person. However, financial protection can ensure that the family does not suffer additional hardship during a difficult time.

Human Life Value helps us understand this responsibility clearly.

When individuals recognise the financial value of their life, they begin to take insurance seriously.

And when insurance professionals truly believe in the purpose of protection, they naturally achieve success in their profession.

That is why the journey always begins with belief.

Final Message

Life is uncertain, but planning can be certain.

Protection planning does not remove risk from life.

It removes financial pain from risk.

A family protected is a confident family.

When you help a family plan protection, you do more than business. You give reassurance, dignity, and stability.

Protection today prevents problems tomorrow.

Secure the income.

Secure the family.

Secure the future.

That is the true purpose of life insurance.

CHAPTER 37

BUILDING LONG-TERM CLIENT RELATIONSHIPS

In the Life Insurance profession, real success does not come from completing many policies in one month. Real success comes from building relationships that continue for many years.

A policy is a temporary business. A relationship is a permanent business.

An agent who depends only on new customers struggles every month. An agent who builds relationships receives continuous business, renewals, and referrals without heavy effort.

1. Treat Clients as People, Not Prospects

Do not see every person only as a policy opportunity. See them as families with responsibilities and emotions. When you genuinely care, customers feel it.

People stay with the person who cares.

2. Regular Contact

Maintain periodic connection:

- Birthday wishes
- Festival greetings
- Important reminders
- Occasional friendly calls

You are not disturbing them. You are staying remembered.

Out of sight becomes out of mind.

Regular contact keeps the connection alive.

3. Annual Review Meeting

Once a year, meet your client and review their situation:

- Income increase
- New child
- Loan taken
- Job change

As life changes, protection needs also change. This naturally leads to additional business.

Service leads to opportunity.

4. Be Available

Respond to calls and messages promptly. If you cannot answer immediately, return the call later. Availability builds reliability.

Reliable agents become preferred advisors.

5. Support During Important Events

Attend or acknowledge important occasions when possible:

- Child admission
- Marriage
- Retirement

Presence strengthens the bond beyond business.

6. Help Without Expectation

Sometimes help without business — guiding a form, giving information, or advising on planning. Customers remember unselfish help.

Service without expectation creates loyalty.

7. Keep Records

Maintain client details:

- Family members
- Policy dates
- Important occasions

Preparedness shows professionalism.

8. Never Disappear After Sale

Many agents contact customers only when they need another policy. This weakens trust. Maintain steady communication even when there is no business discussion.

Consistency builds confidence.

9. Become a Family Advisor

Gradually, customers should feel comfortable consulting you about financial matters. When they trust your advice, they will approach you first.

Advisor status brings automatic business.

10. The Long-Term Benefit

A satisfied client may:

- Continue multiple policies
- Refer relatives and friends
- Seek your advice regularly

One relationship can support your career for years.

Important Understanding

Advertising brings attention.

Relationship brings retention.

Retention is more valuable than acquisition.

Your reputation grows through long-term clients. When your name is associated with reliability, people contact you without hesitation.

Meet respectfully.

Serve sincerely.

Stay connected consistently.

When customers feel you are part of their support system, they do not change their agent.

A good agent gets business.

A trusted agent gets loyalty.

And loyalty creates lifelong success.

CHAPTER 38

PERSONAL BRANDING FOR LIFE INSURANCE AGENTS

In today's world, people prefer to deal with a known and trusted person rather than a stranger. Personal branding means creating a clear and positive identity in the minds of people. When someone in your area thinks about financial protection or insurance, your name should come first.

Branding is not advertising loudly.

Branding is being remembered positively.

You are not only representing a company. You are representing yourself.

1. Define Your Identity

Decide how people should recognise you:

- Family protection advisor
- Child education planner
- Retirement planning guide

When your message is clear, people remember you easily.

2. Consistent Behaviour

Your behaviour in every meeting should be polite, punctual, and professional. Repeated good behaviour builds a reputation.

Reputation is built slowly but remembered strongly.

3. Professional Appearance

Dress neatly and maintain a confident personality. When people repeatedly see you organised and respectful, they automatically associate you with reliability.

Appearance creates perception.

4. Share Knowledge Publicly

You can share useful information:

- Short educational talks
- Community awareness meetings
- Helpful financial tips

Teaching increases trust. People trust those who guide them.

5. Stay Active in Community

Participate in local events, school meetings, and social activities. Visibility increases familiarity. Familiarity increases comfort.

People choose known faces.

6. Use Simple Communication Platforms

Send helpful messages occasionally:

- Financial awareness tips
- Premium reminders
- Planning suggestions

Do not spam. Provide value.

Helpful information creates authority.

7. Maintain Consistency

Branding is not a one-time effort. It is repeated positive action over time. Every interaction contributes to your image.

Consistency creates identity.

8. Protect Your Image

Always speak respectfully and honestly. One negative behaviour can damage many positive impressions.

Your character is your brand.

9. Build Trust Through Service

Helping in claim settlement, guidance, and support strengthens your identity as a dependable advisor.

Service is the strongest promotion.

10. Long-Term Effect

Once your name becomes trusted, new customers approach you through referrals and recognition. You spend less time searching and more time guiding.

Your work becomes easier and more enjoyable.

Important Understanding

Branding does not require a large expense.

It requires consistent sincerity.

People remember the person who helped them understand important decisions.

Become known for honesty.

Become known for helpfulness.

Become known for reliability.

When your name stands for trust, business follows automatically.

Your brand is not your visiting card.

Your brand is your behaviour.

And behaviour repeated daily becomes a reputation.

CHAPTER 39

CONTINUOUS LEARNING AND SELF-IMPROVEMENT

The Life Insurance profession is not a one-time learning career. It is a continuous learning career. Customers today are more informed, more questioning, and more careful before taking decisions. An agent who stops learning slowly loses confidence.

Learning keeps you relevant.

Your knowledge should grow along with your experience.

1. Why Learning is Necessary

Every year:

- Financial awareness increases
- Customer expectations increase
- Communication styles change

If your approach remains old, customers feel disconnected. Learning helps you communicate in a modern and understandable way.

Growth prevents stagnation.

2. Learn From Every Meeting

Every customer interaction teaches something:

What worked well?

Where did the customer hesitate?

Which explanation was clear?

Reflect daily. Experience becomes valuable only when reviewed.

Observation improves skill.

3. Attend Training Programs

Participate in training sessions, workshops, and seminars. Listening to experienced professionals gives new ideas and confidence.

Learning from others reduces mistakes.

4. Read Regularly

Develop a habit of reading:

- Communication skills
- Motivation
- Financial awareness
- Customer psychology

Even 10–15 minutes of daily reading improves thinking and speaking ability.

Reading sharpens expression.

5. Observe Successful Agents

Notice how successful agents:

- Start conversations
- Handle objections
- Maintain relationships

Adopt good practices and adapt them to your personality.

Success leaves clues.

6. Improve Communication Skills

Practice speaking clearly. Learn to explain ideas simply. The more clearly you communicate, the more comfortable customers feel.

Clarity increases acceptance.

7. Upgrade Personal Skills

Work on:

- Confidence
- Listening ability
- Time management
- Patience

Professional success depends on personal development.

You grow first.

Business grows next.

8. Accept Feedback

If a senior, mentor, or even a customer suggests improvement, accept it positively. Feedback shows opportunity for growth.

Correction improves performance.

9. Stay Curious

Ask questions. Seek better ways to explain. Try new methods of approach. Curiosity keeps your work interesting.

Curiosity creates creativity.

10. Never Feel "I Know Enough"

The moment you believe you know everything, improvement stops. The moment you decide to learn continuously, progress starts again.

Learning is a lifelong process.

Important Understanding

Knowledge increases confidence.

Confidence improves communication.

Communication builds trust.

A learning agent becomes a respected advisor.

In this profession, experience gives understanding, and learning gives refinement. Together they create excellence.

Invest time in improving yourself daily. The return will appear in your performance and reputation.

Grow in knowledge.

Grow in skill.

Grow in confidence.

Because an agent who learns continuously succeeds continuously.

CHAPTER 40

BELIEVE FIRST — ACHIEVE NEXT (FINAL MESSAGE)

Every profession gives income, but a few professions give meaning. The life insurance profession gives both.

A Life Insurance agent's journey is not always easy. There will be days when calls are unanswered, meetings are cancelled, and customers postpone decisions. There will be moments of doubt and disappointment. But there will also be moments of gratitude — when a family thanks you for your guidance, when a parent feels relieved about a child's future, and when your effort protects someone from financial hardship.

These moments define the true value of your work.

You are not standing in front of customers only to complete a target. You are standing to create security. Every discussion you have increases awareness. Every policy you complete reduces someone's future worry.

Never underestimate your role.

A doctor saves a life at a critical moment.

A life insurance agent saves a family after a critical moment.

Your words today may become a family's strength tomorrow.

Many agents stop because they lose confidence early. They think success belongs only to a few talented people. But success in this profession does not depend on extraordinary talent. It depends on ordinary actions performed consistently.

Meet people daily.

Speak sincerely.

Serve patiently.

Results may not appear immediately, but they will certainly appear gradually.

There will be rejection. Accept it calmly.

There will be a delay. Handle it patiently.

There will be success. Receive it humbly.

Every successful agent once faced hesitation. Every confident speaker once felt nervous. Confidence did not come before action. Confidence came after repeated action.

Do not wait to become perfect before starting. Start, and improvement will follow.

Your belief about yourself decides your performance. If you believe this profession is difficult, your effort will be reduced. If you believe this profession is meaningful, your dedication increases.

First belief, then behaviour, then result.

Your future in Life Insurance is not decided by market conditions, competition, or contacts. It is decided by your daily discipline, your honesty, and your persistence.

Work in such a way that your name becomes associated with trust. Let people feel comfortable when they see you. Let families feel safe when they speak to you.

One day, you will realise that your success is not only measured by commission, but by the number of families who feel secure because of your guidance.

That is the true achievement.

Keep learning.

Keep meeting people.

Keep serving sincerely.

There will be slow days, but there will also be strong years. Stay patient and consistent. The profession rewards those who continue.

Always remember:

Doubt stops action.

Action builds confidence.

Confidence creates success.

So, believe in your role.

Believe in your effort.

Believe in your purpose.

Because…

Believe First — Achieve Next.

Why do some Life Insurance agents struggle for years while a few agents consistently perform, earn respect, and build a powerful career?

The difference is not luck. The difference is understanding people.

Many agents enter the Life Insurance profession with enthusiasm but slowly lose confidence due to rejection, fear of approaching customers, and lack of proper guidance. They know the plans, they know the premium calculations, yet they hesitate to speak confidently in front of a client. This book is written to solve that exact problem.

Believe First — Achieve Next is not a theory book. It is a practical field guide designed especially for Life Insurance agents. Inside these pages, you will learn:

- How to approach a new customer without fear
- How to start a conversation and build instant trust
- How to create the need for insurance naturally
- How to explain plans in simple language that customers understand

- How to handle objections and rejections confidently
- How to close a policy without pressure
- Daily activity system for continuous performance
- Psychology of customers and decision making
- Ready-to-use communication lines and field examples

This book transforms an agent from a "policy seller" into a "family financial advisor." It will help you not only improve your business but also earn respect, confidence, and long-term relationships with clients.

Remember:

People may postpone investment.

People may postpone luxury.

But they should never postpone protection.

If you truly want to succeed in Life Insurance with honesty, a service mindset, and consistent performance, this book will become your daily companion.

Believe First — Achieve Next

— Sathya Prakash Urs S N

M.Sc., MBA (Ph.D.)

LIC Chief Organiser/Assistant Professor

Motivational Speaker | Trainer | Mentor